football heroes

Chris Martin

Foreword by John Barnes

A GCAP Media & Think Book

THINK
BOOKS

A GCAP Media & Think Book

First published in Great Britain in 2005 by
Think Publishing
The Pall Mall Deposit
124-128 Barlby Road, London W10 6BL
www.thinkpublishing.co.uk

Written by Chris Martin
21st Century Guides team: Christopher Bennett, James Collins, Rica Dearman, Rhiannon
Guy, Emma Jones, James Lamb, Matt Packer, Sonja Patel, Mark Searle, Jes Stanfield,
Lou Millward and Suzi Williams

GCAP Media plc
30 Leicester Square
London WC2H 7LA

ISBN 1-84525-006-0

Printed & bound in Great Britain by William Clowes Ltd, Beccles, Suffolk.

The publishers and authors have made every effort to ensure the accuracy and currency of
the information in Football Heroes. Similarly, every effort has been made to contact
copyright holders. We apologise for any unintentional errors or omissions. The publisher
and authors disclaim any liability, loss, injury or damage incurred as a consequence, directly
or indirectly, of the use and application of the contents of this book.
Cover image: Alamy Images

The rules of soccer are very simple, basically it is this: If it moves, kick it. If it doesn't move, kick it until it does.

Phil Woosnam

THE AUTHORS WOULD LIKE TO THANK:

Even the smallest of books is a collaborative effort, mainly because no writer alive has been able to keep their professional life separate from their personal life. As I am no exception to this rule, heartfelt thanks go to the following for their help and support during the writing of this one:

The Sharky family — Rachel, Dan, Taylor and Dax — for sacrificing family harmony to give me head start.

Bobby and Purdy for keeping me company.

Candy and Finlay for looking after Bobby and Purdy.

Dave, my sometime house guest.

Cousin Bert, Dom, Jessica, Vik and Sara for the commissions which allow me to keep doing what I love for a living.

Hia, Ian, Elena and Denis for keeping my head and my body straight.

The British Library — with the exception of the librarian who told me to stop chewing gum — for the research materials.

Mr, Mrs and Kirsteen Martin as usual.

And Tori, always Tori, for everything.

CONTENTS

INTRODUCTION

The late, great Liverpool manager Bill Shankly once said: 'Football's not a matter of life and death... it's more important than that.' And he was right. For many of us, football is way of life. A passion for some and an inspiration for others. This book is all about those players who've made the beautiful game our national sport and our national obsession.

It's also about remembering that football is more than just 22 men on a pitch. It's the mangers, the referees, the physios, the silverware, the commentators and, of course, the fans. No player can ever forget that the fans are the bedrock of modern football. They pay our wages and they cheer on our teams and this book, I guess, is for them. Here you will find the stories of the players and teams from both home and abroad whose skill and dedication have brought so much joy to so many. Many of the stories are funny, some fill you with awe, others are tragic tales of wasted talent and ruinous bad luck.

Just remembering the greats, Keegan, Pelé, Maradona, Dalglish, Law, Gazza and Best to name a handful, can bring a smile to your face. All together the stories from their outstanding careers put together a fascinating picture of the game today. We love football because it can bring people of all ages, creeds and colours from anywhere in the world together, get them on their feet and get them cheering. That's what football heroes and their accomplishments in those many magical 90 minutes throughout history are all about.

So get out your scarf and rattle for this tribute to all things football, because no matter who you support, you're in for a treat. Enjoy!

John Barnes

The ultimate hero

THE SPECTACULAR RISE AND TERRIBLE FALL OF GEORGE BEST

BEST AT A GLANCE

Full name	**George Best**
Career	**1963:** Makes debut for Manchester United
	1964: Makes debut for Northern Ireland
	1968: Voted European Footballer of the Year
	(the 'Golden Ball' award) and Football Writers'
	Player of the Year
	1970: Sent off for Northern Ireland after throwing
	mud at the referee
	1972: Walks out on Manchester United aged 26
Club and country	Manchester United: 361 appearances, 136 goals
	Northern Ireland: 37 caps, nine goals
Appearances and goals for other teams	Stockport County: three appearances, two goals
	Fulham: 47 appearances, 10 goals
	Hibernian: 22 appearances, three goals
	Bournemouth: five appearances, no goals
Team honours	**1965:** League Championship
	1967: League Championship
	1968: European Cup
Individual honours	Football Writers' Player of the Year (1968)
	European Footballer of the Year (1968)
	Lifetime Achievement Award (2002)
Teams	Manchester United, Stockport County, Cork Celtics,
	Dunstable Town, Los Angeles Aztecs, Fulham, Fort
	Lauderdale Strikers, Hibernian, San Jose Earthquakes,
	Bournemouth, Brisbane Lions

THE SCOUT'S STORY

George Best came from a poor Irish background. The son of a docker and a factory worker, he was one of six children and raised on the Cregagh estate in Belfast. From the moment he could walk, he had a ball at his feet. 'It didn't really matter what sort of ball it was – plastic, a tennis ball, anything I could kick around,' he wrote in *Blessed: My Autobiography*. 'Sometimes, I would even take a ball to bed with me.'

While he showed huge promise as a schoolboy on the football field, his small stature and skinny frame were considered too delicate for the professional game. His break came when Bud MacFarlane, the coach of the Cregagh Boys Club team, pointed Best out to Bob Bishop, who had recently been appointed Manchester United's chief scout for Northern Ireland. The pair arranged a match between Cregagh Boys Club, for whom Best played, and the mighty Boyland Youth Club, run by Bishop. Boyland fielded the finest team in Belfast, made up mainly of boys two or three years older than Best. The game, against heavier, more experienced opponents, was to be a true test of Best's ability. It was a triumph. Best scored twice to lead the Cregagh team to a 4-2 victory.

A few days later Bishop turned up at the Best household and asked the 15-year-old George if he'd like to move to England to play for Manchester United. Best didn't need asking twice. But what the young prodigy didn't know was what Bishop had already reported to Manchester's legendary manager, Sir Matt Busby. Bishop's telegram to the great man had been remarkably prophetic. He simply wrote: 'I think I've found a genius.'

> He was quick, two-footed, beautifully balanced. He could hit long and short passes with equal precision, was swift and fearless in the tackle and he reintroduced the verb 'to dribble'. He was as imaginative and whimsical in midfield as he was economical and deadly given a chance at goal.
> Michael Parkinson

football heroes

GEORGE OF THE ROVERS

When George Best appeared in the *Roy of the Rovers* comic in 13 October 1990, he was asked to named his top five players in the world at that time. He chose:

1. Franco Baresi (AC Milan and Italy)

2. Diego Maradona (Napoli and Argentina)

3. Marco Van Basten (AC Milan and the Netherlands)

4. Pierre Littbarski (Cologne and West Germany)

and Britain's very own

5. Alan Hansen (Liverpool and Scotland)

Roy of the Rovers follows the adventures of Roy Race, star of Melchester Rovers for over half a century. In that time, Roy has lifted every piece of silverware in Europe and even the World Cup. He has captained and managed both Melchester and the England team, played in Spain, the Middle East and the USA. He has survived a terrorist bomb, an earthquake and being shot as well as the death of his wife in a car crash and a coma caused by a helicopter crash. He has taken on hooliganism and the paparazzi, fathered several children and worked as a football pundit. In short, Roy's career has held a mirror to every significant development in the modern game.

THE MANY SIDES OF GEORGE BEST

Just like footballers today, flushed with cash and with an eye for the ladies, Best was a dedicated follower of fashion at a time when collars were wide and trousers were flared. He worked as a model and appeared in adverts adorning everything from eggs and milk to bargain holidays and motor cars. In the late 1960s, he was receiving 10,000 fan mail letters a week and his earnings off the field were more than 10 times his playing salary. Together with Mike Summerbee of Manchester City, George Best opened a number of fashion boutiques in Manchester in 1966 and 1967. He also invested in chief interests and bought a share in a couple of nightclubs, Slack Alice's and Oscar's. Unfortunately, Best's talents were more suited to the pitch as the businesses soon failed.

Best's endlessly sensational existence, love of the high life and precarious finances have meant that this living legend seldom turns down a chance to sell his story for cash. Here are five examples of Best in action on the page...

The Best of Times: My Favourite Football Stories
George Best, Lee Scott
A humorous overview of the game told through anecdotes, insider gossip and tall tales of life in the dressing room and beyond. This is the material that formed the backbone of Best's hugely successful one-man shows and after dinner speeches.

Good, the Bad and the Bubbly
George Best, Ross Benson
A sensationalist ghost-written 'autobiography' in which Best replies to the many tabloid scandals that have dogged him in 'civilian' life. Clearly a book written for the money.

Bestie: A Portrait of a Legend
George Best, Joe Lovejoy
A book that steers a dark passage through Best's failures and frustrations without skimping on the gory details. His troubled relationship with his family in Belfast, his near-adoption by Matt Busby, his tensions with Bobby Charlton and his serious personal failures, both on and off the pitch, are all here.

Blessed: The Autobiography
George Best
A touching and highly personal autobiography in which Best speaks frankly about the alcoholism that shattered his career, bankrupted him and undermined so much of his private life.

Scoring at Half-Time
George Best
Lightweight autobiography that focuses with ready wit on humorous tales from Best's career, gossip and the many beauties that have enjoyed his attentions.

The best player in the world.
Pelé

GEORGE BEST VS TERRY WOGAN

George Best's alcoholism has been a curse that has taken his career, his fortune, several marriages and most painfully of all, his dignity. One such occasion was witnessed by an audience of millions when he appeared drunk on the BBC chat show *Wogan* in 1990.

In *Blessed: The Autobiography*, Best describes himself as already being in the midst of a bender inspired by the return of his son, Callum, to the US. Instructed to arrive at the BBC studios at a certain time, he did so, only to find that he had three hours to kill before the show went live on air. Leaving a thirsty Best alone in a Green Room full of booze wasn't the most sensible thing in the world. By transmission time, he was loaded.

When Terry Wogan asked the great footballer about all the women he'd been out with, Best replied: 'Terry, I like screwing, all right?' The remark sent the producer and the show's host into freefall, the latter desperately back-pedalling and attempting to end the interview before his (obviously inebriated) guest said anything worse. Attempting to change the subject, Wogan asked what Best liked to do with his time since retiring from football. 'Screw,' replied the footballer.

The next day, the tabloid newspapers went into overdrive. Best, watching the tapes of the show, admitted that while he thought he'd been tipsy, in fact he'd been out of it. Wogan initially banned him from the show, realised that his ratings had soared because of the Best appearance, then changed his mind and invited him back. While some were outraged at his offensive language so early in the evening, others found it funny. Most found it sad. This public display marked the nadir of his downfall.

> **I was in for 10 hours and had 40 pints – beating my previous record by 20 minutes.**
> George Best, speaking about a blood transfusion for his liver transplant

THE MOST FEARED BEHIND IN FOOTBALL

George Best turned professional officially in 1963 and made his debut for Manchester United's first team that autumn at home against West Bromwich Albion, who were then sitting right behind the Red Devils at second in the league.

Best quickly quashed fears that his youth and small physique would be no match for older, match-hardened players. He had an impressive first game, the highlight of which was his running rings around West Brom's hugely experienced and much feared full-back, Graham Williams. In one of his first moves on goal, he showed Williams the ball, and then 'nutmegged' him – kicking the ball clean through his legs and picking it up behind him. United won the match 1-0 to keep them top of the table with Best playing a key role in the goal.

Years later Williams came across Best, the pair of them now retired, at an FA function. Williams, on spotting his tormentor, immediately stopped Best in his tracks and said to him: 'Will you stand still for a minute so I can look at your face?' 'Why?' asked the puzzled Best, anticipating the worst. 'Because all I've ever seen of you,' explained Williams, 'is your arse disappearing down the touchline.' A sure sign of the respect that the young Best's trademarked swerve and legendary ball control had earned among the defenders he had terrorised.

George Best is one of the greatest footballers of all time, who brought pleasure to millions over the years.
Gary Lineker

'GEORGIE BEST, SUPERSTAR, WALKS LIKE A WOMAN AND WEARS A BRA!'

It is worth remembering why George Best is so famous. As a footballer, no one had ever seen anything like him. With Manchester United, he won two League championships, the European Cup and was voted European Footballer of the Year. Pelé named him as his favourite player, which was remarkable considering Best's Northern Irish nationality meant he never appeared in the World Cup finals.

Best arrived, aged 15, at a Manchester United still haunted by the spectre of the Munich air crash of 1958. By January 1964, they were fielding a world-class triumvirate of Denis Law, Bobby Charlton and George Best — perhaps the greatest combination in British football. And Best, said the sportswriter David Miller, was a 'fantasy brought to life'.

He immediately bewitched the opposition and beguiled fans in equal measure. A first trophy — the League title — came in 1965. That same season he almost single-handedly dismantled an experienced Benfica side in the European Cup. He scored two goals in the first 15 minutes of the game after being told by the manager Matt Busby to 'keep it tight'. Afterwards, Busby turned to Best and said wryly: 'You obviously weren't listening.'

Two seasons and another domestic title later, Best and United reached the pinnacle of their achievements. Having come back from 3-1 down to beat Real Madrid in the semi-final of the European Cup, United faced Benfica again.

On home soil at Wembley, the match went into extra-time. It was then that Best stepped up with a moment of magic, scoring the goal that gave them an extra-time lead, setting his side en route to a famous 4-1 victory.

A few short years later, Best would disappear off into a journeyman lifestyle of second-grade teams, booze and personal appearances. He claimed that he never had the heart to play for anyone but Manchester United at the top level, but everyone who loved football mourned his decision.

Manager heroes

THE BUCK STOPS HERE

CLOUGHIE KISSES AND MAKES UP

Few managers have been quite as beloved and quite as eccentric as Brian Clough. Born into a working class family on Teesside on 21 March 1935, he became a professional footballer with his local club Middlesbrough at the age of 17. He went on to score an astonishing 204 goals in 222 matches and followed that with 63 goals in 74 matches for Sunderland. He was a swashbuckling centre-forward who even played twice for England in 1959. But 'Cloughie', or 'Old Big 'Ead', as he liked to call himself after receiving an OBE, will always be remembered for his sensational period as a club manager.

He appointed Peter Taylor as his assistant, whose personality provided a vital balance to Clough's extremes. Together they won the League Championship with Derby County in 1972 before taking over at Nottingham Forest in 1975. Forest, then in the Second Division, were League champions within three years and went on to win the European Cup twice.

The latter half of his career was marred by increasing alcohol abuse and his once loveable and eccentric behaviour became erratic in a way that threatened to eclipse his achievements on the field. Clough found himself more than ever head to head with management, football pundits and even the fans in his determination to do things his way.

The most notorious incident came in February 1989, when he was charged with bringing the game into disrepute, fined £5,000 and banned from the touchline of all Football League grounds for an entire season. Clough lashed out at two pitch invaders after a League Cup quarter-final tie, clipping them round the ear and sending them back to the stands. Brought together with the pair for the cameras afterwards, Clough was as typically unbending and loveable as ever. He unconvincingly apologised before grabbing the two in headlocks and demanding: 'Right, now give us a kiss.'

We talk about it for 20 minutes and then we decide I was right.
Brian Clough on management

> **I've told the players we need to win so that I can have the cash to buy some new ones.**
>
> Chris Turner, Peterborough manager, motivates his troops

TOP 10 TRANSFER FEES INVOLVING BRITISH CLUBS

1. **£30 million,** Rio Ferdinand, Leeds to Manchester United, 2002

2. **£28.1 million,** Juan Sebastian Veron, Lazio to Manchester United, 2001

3. **£27 million,** Wayne Rooney, Everton to Manchester United, 2004

4. **£24.4 million,** Michael Essien, Lyon to Chelsea, 2005

5. **£24 million,** Didier Drogba, Marseille to Chelsea, 2004

6. **£21 million,** Shaun Wright-Phillips, Manchester City to Chelsea, 2005

7. **£19 million,** Ruud Van Nistelrooy, PSV Eindhoven to Manchester United, 2001

8. **£18 million,** Rio Ferdinand, West Ham United to Leeds United, 2000

9. **£17.6 million,** Jose Antonio Reyes, Sevilla to Arsenal, 2004

10. **£17 million,** Damien Duff, Blackburn Rovers to Chelsea, 2003

MAKING MANAGEMENT SIMPLE

Shortly after signing the Yugoslav international Ivan Golac, legend has it that Southampton manager Lawrie McMenemy called a team meeting to discuss tactics for a forthcoming game. He began by drawing a diagram of a ball and a goal on a blackboard, speaking very, very slowly as he carefully articulated each play.

Apparently, Alan Ball, the team's then captain, eventually stopped his boss and reminded him that such a heavy-handed presentation was not necessary. 'Ivan speaks perfect English,' he said.

'I'm not doing this for him,' McMenemy replied, 'I'm doing it for the rest of you!'

TEN FAMOUS MILLIONAIRES WHO HAVE OWNED A FOOTBALL TEAM

1. Elton John (Watford)
2. Delia Smith (Norwich)
3. Roman Abramovich (Chelsea)
4. Chris Smith (QPR)
5. Malcolm Glazer (Manchester United)
6. Mohammed Al Fayed (Fulham)
7. David Gold (Birmingham City)
8. Harry Dobson (Manchester United)
9. David Sullivan (Birmingham City)
10. Jack Walker (Blackburn Rovers)

IN THE NICK OF TIME – INCREDIBLE SUBSTITUTIONS

Substituting the right player at the right time can change the course of a club's history. In 1977 Liverpool were going for an unprecedented treble of League, FA Cup and European Cup. In their European Cup quarter-final second-leg against St Etienne at Anfield, the Reds were locked at 2-2 on aggregate, with the French side set to progress on away goals. Enter 'Super Sub' David Fairclough – a player with a reputation for scoring after coming off the bench. He replaced the injured John Toshack as Liverpool pressed for a late winner. With six minutes remaining Fairclough ran onto a lobbed pass, drew the goalkeeper before steering the ball into the net for the winning goal. Two months later Liverpool won their first European Cup, beating Borussia Moenchengladbach 3-1 in Rome, although they fell short in their treble bid, losing the FA Cup final to Manchester United.

Sometimes having a 'hungry' substitute can change a game. One such player was Ian Wright, never a man happy warming the bench. He came on for Crystal Palace who, with only 20 minutes remaining, were 2-1 down against Manchester United in the 1990 FA Cup final. Despite having recently recovered from a broken leg, Wright picked up a cross from Mark Bright and equalised. He scored again in extra time as the game finished a thrilling 3-3 draw.

But if you are looking for instant results, look no further than Gianfranco Zola. Coming on as substitute for Chelsea against VFB Stuttgard in the 1998 European Cup Winners' Cup final, Zola scored an incredible goal after being on the pitch for 18 seconds! It was the goal that won the trophy for the Blues.

THE PEOPLE'S MANAGER – TERRY VENABLES

When people think of the archetypal football manager, more often than not they think of Terry Venables. El Tel (as he became known after a spell managing Barcelona) has set the management template for the last 20 years.

Born in Bethnal Green, London, in 1943, Venables began his professional career as a midfielder for Chelsea in 1960. Nationally, he was the first player to win England honours at every level from schoolboy to full international, being capped twice.

On his retirement from playing, he took over as manager at Crystal Palace, getting them promoted to the First Division in 1979 and building the 'team of the 80s'. He performed the same promotion miracle for QPR in 1983, before leaving for Barcelona in 1984. After leading them to the Spanish title and a European Cup final, he returned to the UK in 1987 to manage Tottenham Hotspur. He led them to an FA Cup victory in 1991, but clashed with the club's owner, Alan Sugar, who dismissed him on the eve of their 1993 FA Cup semi-final, a decision which landed Sugar in the High Court.

By 1994, despite not being involved in management, Venables was the obvious choice to take over the national team, floundering under Graham Taylor. Under Venables England produced some of its best ever football during the 1996 European Championship, before suffering a bitter loss to Germany on penalties in the semi-finals. However, Venables' business interests and burgeoning media career were consuming most of his time and he left the job shortly afterwards. Just as well, for in 1998, he was banned from being a company director for seven years. Venables admitted 19 specific allegations of serious misconduct made against him, including falsified accounting and trading while insolvent.

After spells in different roles at Portsmouth, Crystal Palace and Middlesbrough (he even coached Australia for a while), Venables last gasp came in 2002 when he became manager at Leeds United. The club, however, was already caught in a downward spiral, and unable to stem the decline, Venables left in 2003.

As of 2004 Venables is back as a football pundit on ITV. While some might argue that he has remarkably little silverware for a manager of his reputation, his name remains synonymous with English football.

SHORTEST SPELL AS THE MANAGER OF A TEAM

Three days – Bill Lambton (Scunthorpe United) 1959
Seven days – Tim Ward (Exeter City) 1959
Six days – Kevin Cullis (Swansea City) 1996
10 days – Dave Cowling (Doncaster Rovers) 1997
10 days – Peter Cormack (Cowdenbeath) 2000
13 days – Johnny Cochrane (Reading) 1939
13 days – Mickey Adams (Swansea City) 1997
18 days – Jimmy McIlroy (Bolton) 1970
20 days – Paul Went (Leyton Orient) 1981
27 days – Malcolm Crosby (Oxford) 1998
28 days – Tommy Docherty (QPR) 1968
32 days – Steve Coppell (Manchester City) 1996
42 days – Steve Wicks (Lincoln) 1995
45 days – Jock Stein (Leeds) 1978
44 days – Brian Clough (Leeds) 1974
48 days – John Toshack (Wales) 1994
48 days – David Platt (Southampton) 1999

A CHAIRMAN IN SEVENTH HEAVEN

In August 2003, the chairman of Scottish Second Division team Airdrie United, Jim Ballantyne, announced that in the light of a recent visit with several friends to Glasgow's Seventh Heaven strip club, his team was to be sponsored by it. Players running on to the pitch, he ruled, would be greeted by billboards depicting scantily-clad strippers. 'I rank it as one of my greatest achievements since I took over at Airdrie United,' Ballantyne declared. 'Sexy football is coming to Airdrie United one way or another; I will be the only chairman in Scottish football who'll still be in seventh heaven, even if we get gubbed 4-0 on a Saturday!'

Ballantyne was true to his word. The hoardings at the club's New Broomfield ground were soon advertising Seventh Heaven as 'The Chairman's Choice.'

FOOTBALL'S HIGHEST PAID COACHES TO DATE

1. Jose Mourinho, Chelsea, €7.5 million (£5.1 million)

2. Alex Ferguson, Manchester United, €6 million (£4.1 million)

3. Sven-Goran Eriksson, England, €5.8 million (£3.9 million)

4. Arsene Wenger, Arsenal, €4.4 million (£3 million)

5. Ottmar Hitzfeld, ex-Bayern Munich, €3.3 million (£2.2 million)

6. Fabio Capello, Juventus, €3.2 million (£2.2 million)

7. Jürgen Klinsmann, Germany, €3.1 million (£2.1 million)

8. Claudio Ranieri, ex-Valencia, €2.9 million (£2 million)

9. Rafael Benitez, Liverpool, €2.6 million (£1.8 million)

10. Alberto Zaccheroni, ex-Internazionale, €2.3 million (£1.6 million)

SVEN GORAN ERIKSSON: PASSION FOR SOCCER

Managing England must be one of the hardest jobs in the footballing world, trying to pull a solid performance from a squad of highly paid, egotistical players and, worst of all, trying to satisfy the expectations of a notoriously unforgiving nation. Swede Sven-Goran Eriksson has been the steady hand behind the white shirts since 2000. But for all the passion the game arouses, he is not given to unbridled public displays of emotion. Indeed, it was said of Eriksson that his idea of a celebration was to raise both eyebrows simultaneously.

So it came as a shock to discover that bachelor Eriksson is a demon in the bedroom. In the wake of high-profile affairs with TV presenter Ulrika Jonsson and FA secretary Faria Alam, his long time girlfriend Nancy Dell'Olio revealed a remarkable nugget about Sven's bedroom technique in *GQ* magazine. The manager of England's national soccer team recites the names of his squad during sex.

'It's the whole squad,' she told the magazine. 'All 22!'

> ## I wanted someone I could rely on when the fists were flying in the dressing room.
>
> Bobby Robson, on why he selected
> Bobby Ferguson as his assistant.

KARREN BRADY – A WOMAN WITH BALLS

Karren Brady's appointment as Managing Director of Birmingham City in 1993 was a unique appointment in the male chauvinist world of English football. Not only was she a woman entering a male-dominated world, but she was also hired by the diminutive publisher of pornography, David Sullivan.

Indeed Brady started as a reporter on Sullivan's *Sport* 'newspaper', working her way up to editor before her surprise appointment at the head of the magnate's latest concern, Birmingham City FC. Of the change, Brady said: 'I met much more chauvinism when I was working for the *Sport*. I've always had the "I bet she's shagging the boss" remarks.'

She settled for 'shagging' a player instead, striker Paul Peschisolido. She said: 'I'd stop working tomorrow if I became Paul's wife. I love what I do, but my place would be at home for him. I know that that will come as a shock to people who assume I'm a feminist, but I'm an old-fashioned girl and I truly believe that a wife should cook, clean and stay at home and look after kids.' Of course, when she married Peschisolido, Brady promptly... remained as managing director of Birmingham City. She was subsequently involved in transferring her husband because it wasn't working out... for footballing, not romantic reasons. The couple are still together.

In her 12 years at Birmingham, Brady has worked alongside strong-minded managers Barry Fry, Trevor Francis and Steve Bruce and has overseen Birmingham's rise from the old Division One to the Premiership where they are now established. Of her managerial style she once said: 'I know people in the game prefer to deal with me because I am tough and uncompromising. Barry Fry can be like Father Christmas. I am like a wicked stepmother.'

FIVE FOOTBALL MANAGERS WHO HAVE RECEIVED KNIGHTHOODS

1. Sir Matt Busby
2. Sir Alex Ferguson
3. Sir Walter Winterbottom
4. Sir Alf Ramsey
5. Sir Bobby Robson

KEVIN KEEGAN – ALL ABOUT THE SPIRIT

Kevin Keegan had an exceptional playing career, typified by enthusiasm and spirit. Famously, when he fell from a bicycle while competing in the BBC's *Superstars*, he picked himself up and went on to continue the race. This was the Keegan spirit. It was something he looked for in others as a manager, but seldom found. The result was disappointment and short tenures at the very highest levels.

As a player Keegan found fame with Liverpool, particularly during the 1976-1977 season, when Keegan was instrumental in Liverpool's charge towards an unprecedented 'treble' of League championship, FA Cup and European Cup. After eight years of retirement and golf in Spain, Keegan returned to the game as manager of Newcastle United. During Keegan's reign as manager, Newcastle finished runners-up to Manchester United in the Premiership in 1996. It was during this time that Keegan launched an infamous tirade on Sky Sports. Manchester United manager Alex Ferguson had suggested that teams made more of an effort against Manchester United than Newcastle United. After Newcastle's hard-won victory over Leeds United in their next game, an emotional Keegan said: 'I think you have to send a tape of the game to Alex Ferguson – isn't that [the Leeds performance] he wants?'

The rant came as Newcastle lost its previous 12-point lead at the top of the Premiership. Manchester United duly collected the title once again but, undoubtedly, most people outside Old Trafford wanted Newcastle to win.

THE MANY SIDES OF ALEX FERGUSON

Alex Ferguson was born in Govan, then a slum area in Glasgow, on 31 December 1941. From these humble roots he rose through the ranks of the footballing world, first as a player and then as a manager. However, Alex Ferguson is not just any manager – his huge success at Manchester United has included achieving a double, a double double and, in 1999, an awe-inspiring treble.

His playing career started at Queen's Park in 1958 and included spells for St Johnstone, Dunfermline, Rangers, Falkirk and Aberdeen. Before managing Manchester United he briefly took the helm at East Sterling, St Mirren and even helped Aberdeen to the European Cup Winners Cup in 1983. He was also briefly in charge of Scotland's national side in 1986. That same year he joined Manchester United, where he has been ever since, guiding the team with legendary psychological skill, canny purchases and good tactics, helping the club become the powerhouse it is today.

But there's more to Alex Ferguson than football. An avid horse-racing fan, he enjoyed a record-breaking seven Group 1 victories with Rock Of Gibraltar, whom he owned in partnership with Sue Magnier, the wife of significant Manchester United shareholder, John Magnier. The horse's success sent its stud price skyrocketing – someone stood to make a fortune, and it was this that began a long-running dispute linked to stud rights between Ferguson and Magnier's Coolmore Stud.

Despite the high-living world that he inhabits, Ferguson has never lost his interest in politics or his roots. Ferguson wrote in *The Mirror* on 12 April 2005: 'I am almost as passionate about politics as I am about football. I have never forgotten where I come from or how fortunate I have been to get where I have – and how important politics has been in improving the lives of the people I come from. I want as many people as possible to have the same chance through hard work to make the most of their talent.'

Ferguson has written an autobiography called *Managing My Life*. Racehorse owner, professional footballer, manager extraordinaire and knight of the realm since 1999. Would that we could all manage our lives as well as Alex Ferguson.

Stretcher heroes

ACHES, BREAKS AND HEADACHES
IN THE LAND OF THE MAGIC SPONGE

SCOTTISH STRIKER STRUCK

During a tight match one day, the story goes that Partick Thistle manager John Lambie was informed that one of his strikers had sustained a concussion and did not know who he was.

Lambie thought for while, then said: 'That's great. Tell him he's Pelé and get him back on!'

> **Football is all very well as a game for rough girls, but is hardly suitable for delicate boys.**
> **Oscar Wilde**

WHAT'S THAT ON YOUR HEAD?

Of all the injuries footballers have to suffer in their career, perhaps the worst of them are those which are self-inflicted. And, without doubt, the very worst of these self-inflicted injuries is the footballer's haircut. Here then is the combination of vanity, fashion and pure insanity that has led to our choice of the top 10 stupid footballers' haircuts:

1. Bobby Charlton's comb over
2. Peter Beardsley's equally ugly pudding-bowl
3. Kevin Keegan's legendary 1970s perm
4. Chris Waddle's mullet
5. Paul Gascoigne's space-age platinum-blond hair extensions
6. Carlos Valderrama's blond mega-afro – proving that follicle madness is not a purely British affair
7. Trifon Ivanov's funky medieval shag
8. Ivan Campo's curly mop
9. Jason Lee's ambitious pineapple cut
10. Ronaldo's Tintin wedge

Looking at this rap sheet for crimes against hair, you can see why FIFA put Pierluigi Collina in charge...

DEATH OF THE BABES – THE MUNICH AIR DISASTER

The Munich air disaster happened on 6 February 1958, when a charter aircraft – British European Flight 609, carrying players and backroom staff from Manchester United plus a number of journalists and supporters – crashed in a blizzard on its third attempt to take off from Munich-Riem airport.

United were returning from Belgrade where they had just edged out Red Star Belgrade in a European Cup quarter-final and had stopped off at Munich for re-fuelling.

Twenty-three of the 43 passengers on board the aircraft lost their lives in the disaster and it devastated the young, potentially world-beating Manchester team, which included the prodigy Duncan Edwards. The team was known as the first generation of the Busby Babes. These were the youth-based teams of legendary manager Sir Matt Busby, spotted early and raised in his unique footballing tradition.

The crash resulted in mass grief and sorrow throughout the footballing world and particularly in the UK. The slow recovery of Matt Busby, the Manchester United manager, was watched intently and reported by the newspapers as he later dragged a threadbare United team through the rest of the 1957-1958 season. Eventually, Busby rebuilt a second generation of Busby Babes, including George Best, who went on to hit the heights that their forebears seemed destined for – namely winning the European Cup in 1968.

This victory did little to ease the pain of the disaster – indeed, the crash became locked in the popular consciousness as a symbol of wasted youth, and one of Manchester's favourite sons, Morrissey, has recorded a song about it.

Those who survived, including Bobby Charlton and Sir Matt Busby himself, would be haunted by it for the rest of their careers.

> **Hoddlesden (n.) - An 'injured' footballer's limp back into the game which draws applause but doesn't fool anybody.**
> Douglas Adams, in his book *The Meaning of Liff*

TOP 10 AVERAGE ATTENDANCES AT
WORLD CUP FINALS TOURNAMENTS

1. 1994 USA – 68,604

2. 1950 Brazil – 60,772

3. 1970 Mexico – 52,311

4. 1966 England – 50,458

5. 1990 Italy – 48,368

6. 1986 Mexico – 46,956

7. 1974 West Germany – 46,684

8. 1998 France – 43,366

9. 1978 Argentina – 42,374

10. 2002 Japan/S Korea – 42,274

**The mere fact that he's injured stops him getting injured again,
if you know what I mean.**
Terry Venables

LINEKER'S CLEAN SWEEP

Match of the Day presenter, former England and Tottenham star and the face of Walker's crisps, Gary Lineker has a whiter-than-white image. Indeed, throughout his entire professional career Lineker was never once booked. But although he could control his temper, he was once rather less successful with his bowel.

During a European Championship match against Ireland in 1998, Lineker unwisely took to the field with an upset stomach. Within 10 minutes, he had soiled more than his reputation.

Cleverly, he attempted to disguise the problem in his shorts by launching into a dramatic sliding tackle against the next available opponent, wiping his backside on the grass as he did so.

SMELLING GOOD, FEELING BAD

Santiago Canizares, Spain's then 32-year-old goalkeeper, was ruled out of the 2002 World Cup after he ruptured a tendon in his foot. Was it the result of a daring clash in the penalty box with an opposition attacker? No such luck. The Spaniard sustained the injury while shaving when he dropped a bottle of cologne on his foot.

> **I think football would become an even better game if someone could invent a ball that kicks back.**
>
> Eric Morecambe

TEN WEIRDEST INJURIES

Damian Spencer (Cheltenham) injured his knees and split open his hand tripping over a plastic dog bone and falling down some stairs.

John Durnin (Portsmouth) dislocated his elbow in a golf-buggy crash.

Robbie Keane (Wolves) damaged his ankle by treading on a TV remote-control handset.

Mark Kennedy (Liverpool) damaged the tendons in his hand by pulling on a training-ground bib.

Celestine Babayro (Chelsea) broke his ankle performing a celebratory somersault in a pre-season warm-up match.

Alan Wright (Aston Villa) developed a knee problem as a result of the position of the accelerator in his £50,000 Ferrari.

Allan Nielsen (Tottenham Hotspur) was temporarily blinded when his baby daughter poked him in the eye.

Michael Stensgaard (Liverpool) injured his shoulder trying to stop an ironing board from falling over.

Steve Morrow (Arsenal) broke his arm when teammate Tony Adams picked him up as part of a goal celebration.

John Terry (Chelsea) wrenched his ankle while watching Wimbledon.

THE TATTOOS OF DAVID BECKHAM

Not strictly an injury but they must have hurt. Ow!

1. Brooklyn Across his lower back in Gothic script.
2. Guardian angel A human figure with arms outstretched across his shoulders and down his spine. He then added wings to the angel, followed by his second son's name, Romeo, added just above the figure's head.
3. Victoria On the inside of his left forearm in Hindi, followed by the Latin phrase *Ut Amem Et Foveam* added under the name, translating as 'so that I love and cherish'.
4. VII On the inside right forearm – his player number for Manchester United and for England. Then he added *Perfectio In Spiritu* under the number, another Latin phrase, this one meaning 'spiritual perfection'.
5. Angel On his right shoulder and bicep, along with text reading 'In the face of adversity'.
6. Winged cross Controversial and highly visible, on the back of the neck.

All of Beckham's skin art has been done by highly respected Manchester tattooist, Louis Malloy.

COMMON SOCCER INJURIES

1. Lower leg – ankle sprains, shin splints, compartment syndrome

2. Knee – anterior cruciate ligament injury, cartilage meniscus tear

3. Thigh – contusion, muscle strain, pulled hamstring

4. Groin – groin strain, hernia

5. Shoulder – acromioclavicular (AC) joint sprain

SKY SAVES PLAYER'S MODESTY

A curious caption relating to Irish defender Gary Breen was broadcast on *Sky Sports News* in 2001. The item read: 'Gary Breen ruled out for Republic because of a groin stain...'

Referee heroes

THE MEN IN BLACK

REFEREE ABUSE ON THE RISE SAYS UEFA

Referee abuse is on the rise, revealed soccer bosses, UEFA, in 2005. But why the sudden increase in pitch-side abuse?

While some blame the rise of abuse or declining sportsmanship in soccer, including the routine of feigning injury to deceive the referee, others say big business and TV coverage is to blame. Now that televised football has scores of camera crews covering major games, endless angles from which to review controversial decisions in slow-motion are possible. The poor old referee, by contrast, is alone in making his split-second judgements, enjoying occasional help from a linesman but with no recourse to the video replays. What's more, a single goal can cost top-end clubs millions of pounds in revenues.

But referees are reporting difficulties even at the youth level, where matches are watched only by a handful of spectators on the touchlines. Verbal threats from over enthusiastic soccer dads are forcing more referees out of the game. Referees are reported as saying that 'the physical presence in public parks is much more threatening' than a few emails.

'At grass-roots level, fewer people want to become referees,' said Volker Roth, chairman of UEFA's Referees' Committee in March 2005. 'Who is going to do that if you are going to be abused?' Unfortunately for referees, UEFA sees 'no obvious solution' to the problem.

It was like the ref had a brand new yellow card and wanted to see if it worked.
Richard Rufus

THE ITALIANS VS THE REFEREE

At what point does football fanaticism become plain bad sportsmanship? This question was put to the test in South Korea's 2002 World Cup quarter-final match against Italy. With just a few minutes of playing time left, a defensive mistake gave the Koreans an equaliser. Seconds later, the Italian striker Christian Vieri was presented with an unmissable chance to settle the match. He missed and the match went into an extra-time golden goal period (in which the game ends as soon as anyone scores). This went badly for the Italians.

First, an Italian goal was disallowed because of a bad offside decision. Then Francesco Totti, one of Italy's most popular players, was shown the red card for taking a dive. Finally, the Korean striker Ahn Jung-Hwan headed a last-gasp winner. The disputed decisions, and the loss of the game were all the Italian nation needed to come to the entirely illogical decision. It was all the referee's fault.

The FIFA email system crashed after receiving an estimated four hundred thousand enraged messages about the referee's decisions. Franco Frattini, the Italian minister for public offices, described the referee as 'a disgrace, absolutely scandalous' and implied he had been bribed. The referee in question, Byron Moreno, of Ecuador, perhaps unwisely suggested that the accusations of bribery were a bit rich, coming from a country not unfamiliar with the concept itself. This was the final straw. In Rome, the public prosecutor's office promptly opened an investigation into Moreno's conduct. TV stations, prosecutors and government ministers all joined in the referee witch hunt... at one stage it seemed as if Italy was coming close to declaring actual war on Ecuador.

The person who actually lost Italy the match, the Korean striker who scored the decisive goal, Ahn Jung-Hwan, didn't get off lightly either. He had been playing his club football in Perugia, Italy. Luciano Gaucci, the president of the Perugia football club promptly announced that Ahn was fired. 'That gentleman will never set foot in Perugia again,' Gaucci said. 'I have no intention of paying a salary to someone who has ruined Italian soccer.'

TOP 10 UK PLAYERS WITH MOST LEAGUE APPEARANCES

1. Peter Shilton (1966-1997) – **1,005**

2. Tony Ford (1975-2002) – **931**

3. Graeme Armstrong (1975-2001) – **909**

4. Tommy Hutchison (1965-1991) – **863**

5. Terry Paine (1957-1977) – **824**

6. Neil Redfearn (1982-2004) – **790**

7. Robbie James (1973-1994) – **782**

8. Alan Oakes (1959-1984) – **777**

9. John Burridge (1968-1996) – **771**

10. John Trollope (1960-1980) – **770**

I never comment on referees, and I'm not going to break the habit of a lifetime for that prat!

Ron Atkinson

HIGHEST NUMBER OF CARDS GIVEN OUT IN A SINGLE GAME

According to the *Guinness Book of Records*, the highest number of red cards awarded in one game, was 20. The cards were handed out by the referee in a League match in Paraguay. after an on-pitch brawl.

Following a close second, referee Antonio Lopez Nieto handed out 18 cards (16 yellow and two red) in a World Cup match between Germany and Cameroon in 2002.

Meanwhile Kenon Howley awarded 10 cards in a 1962 FA Cup match after the entire Mansfield team (minus keeper) lined up and sarcastically applauded him for giving Crystal Palace a penalty.

WORLD CUP REFEREE RECORDS

Youngest referee
Francisco Matteucci (Uruguay) – 27 years and 62 days in 1930

Oldest referee
George Reader (England) – 53 years and 236 days in 1950

Fastest sending off
Jose Batista (Uruguay) – 56 seconds against Scotland in 1986

Fastest yellow card to a player in finals
Sergei Gorlukovich (Russia) – booked after one minute in a match
against Sweden in 1994

First player to be sent off
Mario de Las Casas (Peru) – in a match against Romania in 1930
*The red and yellow card system didn't come into use until 1970. The first
player to be given the red card was Chile's Carlos Caszely in a match
against West Germany in 1974. The first player to receive a yellow card was
Lovchev of the USSR in the 1970 opening match against Mexico.*

Only player to have been sent off in successive finals tournaments
Rigobert Song (Cameroon) – sent off against Brazil in 1994
and against Chile in 1998

Fastest red card to a substitute
Marco Etcheverry (Bolivia) – sent off three minutes after being
substituted in during the match against Germany in 1994

First goalkeeper to be sent off
Gianluca Pagliuca (Italy) – in a match against Norway in 1994

Youngest player to have been sent off in finals
Cameroon's Rigobert Song (see above) – 17 years and 358 days old when
sent off in the match against Brazil in 1994

Oldest player to have been sent off in finals
Fernando Clavijo (USA) –aged 37 when sent off in the match against
Brazil in 1994

football heroes

REF'S WHISTLE

The soccer referee's whistle was introduced in 1878. Prior to this a referee had to rely on waving a handkerchief.

THE BIG BALD MAN TAKES TO THE SMALL PITCH

The goulish looking, bald headed Pierluigi Collina is the most famous referee in the world. The renowned official, who has handled many memorable games, including the 2002 World Cup final and the 1999 Champions League final, is so popular that despite reaching the official UEFA retirement age of 45, the Italian FA changed its retirement age so he could referee for another year. But in August 2005 he retired anyway after a sponsorship deal caused a conflict of interest with his refereeing. However, Collina received perhaps the ultimate footballing accolade in 2005 when a table football shop in Wales immortalised him as a Subbuteo figure.

The shop's proud owner Tom Taylor, from Knighton in Powys, has sold around 40 mini versions of the instantly recognisable Italian whistle man. Despite being the world's most beloved table football game, Subbuteo does not sell sets of refs. So Taylor stepped in to satisfy demand from his customers. 'My first attempt didn't look like Collina at all', he said. 'Well, he had a bald head – that was about it.' But a second revamped figure in a revised pose, with whistle raised and arm outstretched, was instantly recognisable. Taylor's set of UEFA mini-size referees comes with Collina and three assistants. It is not the first time Taylor has taken to the workshop to satisfy Subbuteo fans' craving for realism. Two years previously he produced a set of streakers.

I believe in the traditional role of accepting decisions as part of discipline of sportsmanship and fair play.
Pierluigi Collina

KEN ASTON – THE FATHER OF MODERN REFEREEING

You may never have heard of Ken Aston but without him the game of football would be very different and considerably more unruly. Aston was an English teacher and a soldier but primarily a football referee, who was responsible for many of the most important developments in football refereeing.

Aston qualified as a referee in 1936, working his way through the leagues becoming a Football League linesman in the 1949-50 season and then becoming a League referee, before the outbreak of World War II slowed his footballing ambitions.

On his return from military service in 1946, he returned to refereeing, becoming the first League referee to wear the black uniform with white trim. The following year he introduced the bright yellow flags still used by linesmen today.

In 1953, Aston progressed to refereeing senior League matches. He is perhaps best known for refereeing the notorious battle of Santiago, the match between Chile and Italy in the 1962 World Cup, which saw the two teams at each others throats from the first whistle,

and one player cautioned within seconds. Aston was soon after appointed to the FIFA Referees Committee. He served on it for eight years, chairing it for four of those. His experience in refereeing international games where communication could be difficult, led him to devise the system of showing a yellow card for a caution and a red card for a sending-off, which was first used in the 1970 World Cup.

In 1966 Aston also introduced the practice of naming a substitute referee and successfully proposed that the pressure of the ball be specified in the Laws of the Game. In 1974 he introduced the number board for substitutes, so that players could easily see who was being substituted.

Towards the end of his extraordinary career, he became a senior lecturer on the Football Association Referees' Panel and chief instructor for the American Youth Soccer Organisation.

In 1997 his outstanding contribution to the game was rewarded when he received the MBE 'for services to US soccer.'

REF ON THE RUN — ANDERS FRISK FEARS FOR HIS LIFE

It seems ironic that a referee, who has put so much effort into being impartial on the field, should be blamed by supporters when things don't go the way of their team. Such is the story of Anders Frisk, a world class referee for whom the irrational brio of the crowd finally became too much.

Since 1991, Frisk has refereed at the highest level at games all around the world. Respected amongst his peers, the Italian referee, Pierluigi Collina, wrote in his autobiography that Frisk was the only other official he considered to have the credentials to referee a World Cup final.

In 2000, Frisk officiated the European Championship final between France and Italy; an appointment that 'brought me out in goose bumps,' he was later quoted as saying. Now at the forefront of the European refereeing scene, Frisk also took charge of two matches in the World Cup in Japan and Korea.

But on September 15 2004, Frisk was to confront the darker side of modern soccer. He was forced to abandon a match he was refereeing between AS

Roma and Dynamo Kiev at the Stadio Olimpico after he was hit by a missile thrown from the stands as he walked off the field at half-time. Bleeding heavily, he ended the game.

But things would get worse. During a 2005 Champions League tie between FC Barcelona and Chelsea FC, he sent off Chelsea's Didier Drogba for receiving two cautions. Not only did Chelsea criticise Frisk openly for the decision but they publicly accused him of favouritism and cheating when they claimed that Frisk had (irregularly) invited Barcelona manager Frank Rijkaard into his room at half-time. The accusations were entirely untrue.

UEFA charged Chelsea with inappropriate conduct following the match. But the damage had been done. The fans took Chelsea at their word and reacted with terrifying vitriol towards Frisk. On 12 March 2005 Frisk announced his immediate retirement, citing threats made to his family.

The football world lost a great talent and had its eyes opened to the sometimes terrifying world of the man in the black shirt.

FASTEST SENDINGS OFF IN FOOTBALL

0 secs – Walter Boyd
Boyd came on as a substitute for Swansea in a match against Darlington in November 1999. He clashed with Martin Grey while taking position, cuffed him and was promptly sent back off the pitch

10 secs – Giuseppe Lorenzo
Right after kick off, Bologna's Lorenzo struck a Parma player

13 secs – Kevin Pressman
In August 2000 the Sheffield Wednesday keeper was shown the red card for handling the ball outside the penalty area. Fastest in the UK

15 secs – Simon Rea
Peterborough's Rea was off after pulling back a Cardiff player in a 2002 game. Vinnie Jones equalled the record in 2002 during a celebrity match in the US for Hollywood United

52 secs – Ian Culverhouse
Swindon's Culverson handled a goal-bound ball in a game against Everton in 1997. Fastest in the FA Cup

56 secs – Jose Batista
The Uruguay player fouled Scotland's Gordon Strachen in a 1986 World Cup clash. Fastest in the World Cup

72 secs – Tim Flowers
Blackburn keeper brought down Brian Deene of Leeds in the box. Fastest in the Premiership

YOU'VE GOT MAIL – THE FANS VS URS MEIER

Swiss born football referee, Urs Meier is another official who has been at the sharp end of fan reaction to controversial decisions made on the field. Meier's qualifications are impeccable, from 1994 until 2004 he served as an international FIFA referee. He was elected by an expert jury to be the second-best referee in the world in 2002 and third-best in 2004. He officiated at both the 1998 and the 2002 World Cups as well as most of the European championships over the last 20 years.

In his long career two matches have particularly stood out. In both, Meier was forced to make controversial decisions and suffered savage fan reprisals as a result.

The first was a qualification match for Euro 2004 between Romania and Denmark, when Meier awarded a disputed penalty kick to Denmark and let play go on for much longer than the amount of time added on originally by the fourth official. In the extra three minutes play added by Meier, Denmark equalised; a goal which eliminated Romania from the contest. The Romanian press and fans were furious. Several Romanian newspapers published his email address and he received over

14,000 angry emails. Several petitions, signed by thousands of people, were sent to UEFA demanding his dismissal. They were, of course, disregarded.

Further controversy followed in the Euro 2004 quarterfinal between England and Portugal. With the score at 1-1, he disallowed a goal by Sol Campbell in the 89th minute of the game, due to a perceived foul by John Terry on the Portuguese goalkeeper, Ricardo Pereira. The match ended in a tie, and Portugal proceeded to the next stage following a penalty shootout. This time, it was the turn of the English 'fans' to react angrily. Meier's personal details were again published, this time by a British tabloid newspaper. Meier received chilling death threats, more than 16,000 abusive emails and even had an English flag placed outside his home. As a result, the long-suffering referee was placed under police protection.

Despite the inconvenience and menace of such crowd reaction, Urs Meier continued to receive FIFA appointments and referee in the Swiss top division until he reached the mandatory retirement age for each (45) – a solid example of a man who would not bow to intimidation.

Footballers' wives

THE CLOTHES, THE JEWELLERY...
OH YEAH, AND THE WIVES

> **I loved football. I played in the morning and in the afternoon. Even when I went to bed with my wife I was training.**
> Diego Maradona

FIVE HAIRCUTS OF DAVID BECKHAM

1. Full shave ('number one')

2. Hoxton fin

3. Cornrows (with braids)

4. Long and lovely (with Alice band)

5. Mowhawk

It seems Beckham style is not just influencing the hair on our heads. In 2002, it was reported that David Beckham's haircuts were being copied by growing numbers of Japanese women, who were styling their pubic hair in honour of the great man.

The three basic cuts were:

1. Soft Beckham – The hair is allowed to grow freely but curls back to form a natural peak)

2. Popular Beckhams – The hair is brushed into a Mohican

3. Hardcore Beckham – The same as above but the top of the Mohican is dyed an eye-catching colour.

> **Love is good for footballers, as long as it is not at half-time.**
> **Richard Moller Nielsen**

FIVE FOOTBALL PLAYERS WHO MOONLIGHT AS MALE MODELS

1. **David Beckham** (Real Madrid) – Police sunglasses

2. **Freddie Ljungberg** (Arsenal) – Calvin Klein underwear

3. **Cristiano Ronaldo** (Manchester United) – Pepe Jeans

4. **Rio Ferdinand** (Manchester United) – Ben Sherman shirts

5. **David James** (Manchester City) – H&M clothing

GERMAN WOMEN GET IT OFF THEIR CHESTS

After heading the goal which brought a 1-0 victory for Portugal against Holland during Euro 2004, Portuguese star Cristiano Ronaldo tore off his shirt to the cheers of the spectators who packed the stadium. He was promptly given a yellow card by the referee, who declared that Ronaldo's show of flesh constituted 'unsportsmanlike conduct'.

The referee's action was a precedent that football, football players, and loving women across Europe would not stand for. In July of that year, two German Green party MPs, Evelin Schoenhut-Keil and Margareta Wolf, tabled a motion in the German parliament demanding that soccer players be allowed to show off their bodies without getting a yellow card.

The women's motion found vocal support across Germany. Thousands of German woman backed a petition demanding that FIFA rules be changed to allow footballers to rip off their shirts and parade their torsos after a winning goal.

In an open letter to the German Football Association, the two MPs summarised the women's position:

'Get rid of the yellow card and instead let players show their athletic torsos! We can't understand how the voluntary showing of a gorgeous male chest can be objectionable.' Right on, girls.

football heroes

FOOTBALLERS' WIVES – SMALL SCREEN SIRENS

Premiering on ITV in January 2002, the wildly successful show, *Footballers' Wives*, hit a new low (or high, depending how you like your television) in television drama.

Following the daily lives of the beautiful and filthy rich wives of the players at the fictional club Earls Park, the show was a breakneck cavalcade of cat fights, extramarital sex and unchecked brand name flashing. Aside from ludicrous plotting and soap style clichés, the show, while showing virtually no interest in football did root itself in the tabloid reality of the modern game. Walking a thin line with the libel courts, *Footballer's Wives*' stylised plot lines were based on current events and gossip so real that it was hard for viewers not to believe that the show's creators knew something that they didn't. Likewise, the show was packed with characters who were thin and obvious caricatures of the real people who inspired them.

Despite the show's tackiness and its conspicuous celebration of wealth, it wasn't long before real footballers were shooting cameos in it and the show's position in the firmament of modern football was assured.

'The audience of *Footballers' Wives* now have huge expectations for the series, both in terms of story lines and also of the on-screen glamour, we hope to have exceeded these expectations,' said Cameron Roach, the show's producer. And, so far, they have.

While real life footballer's wives, especially those married to jobbing league players, might live suburban lives that are a million miles way from Tanya, Conrad and Amber's antics, everyone prefers the idea that this is truly how is...

> **People say footballers have terrible taste in music but I would dispute that... In the car at the moment I've got The Corrs, Cher, Phil Collins, Shania Twain and Rod Stewart.**
>
> Andy Gray

There is more to being a true footballer's wife than just looking good and sitting in the friends and family box at games. You need to attract tabloid interest. The tabloids are a great paradox, everybody hates them yet everyone reads them. In terms of football, they provide informed sports coverage but more importantly they play a vital part in creating the mythology around footballers' lives. As much as football fans may say they dislike all the sleaze, deep down they're addicted to the gossip. Real life truly is stranger than fiction.

David and Victoria Beckham
With Victoria spending much of her time in England, still trying to re-start her music career, and David playing in Spain, all kinds of allegations have been levelled at Mr Beckham – from energetic sex pest texting to a full-blown affair with his PA Rebecca Loos. All these allegations were strenuously denied by the couple (and their lawyers). Since the Rebecca Loos story broke in 2004, Posh has given birth to her third child, Cruz.

Mark Bosnich and
Sophie Anderton
Former Chelsea goalkeeper Mark and *I'm a Celebrity...* TV star Sophie had a roller coaster relationship, before their much-publicised drugs battles led to an eventual split. Since then, Sophie has overcome her cocaine addiction and enjoyed a relationship with nightclub owner Mark Alexiou before dumping him in August 2005. When Mark B claimed

in the tabloids that he'd enjoyed a steamy reunion with Sophie, Mark A rubbished the claims, saying Mark B was 'lower than the bugs Sophie had eaten in the jungle'.

Wayne Rooney and
Coleen McLoughlin
The England star and his fiancée enjoyed a well-earned holiday in Barbados shortly after his outstanding performance at Euro 2004. A week later, prostitute Charlotte Glover told the tabloids that she'd slept with the Everton striker soon after he had started seeing Coleen. Coleen reacted by maxing out Wayne's credit cards on a legendary shopping trip to New York.

Kate Lawler and
Jonathan Woodgate
Big Brother 3 winner Kate Lawler linked up with Jonathan Woodgate, shortly after his shock move from Newcastle to Real Madrid. The couple

became engaged and and planned a lavish Las Vegas wedding, but they split up in April 2005.

Michael Owen and Louise Bonsall
Along with David Beckham and Jonathan Woodgate, Michael Owen makes up the high-profile trio of England stars who decamped to Real Madrid. Unlike the Beckhams' move, however, Michael's fiancée Louise moved out to Spain with him from the start, along with their little daughter Gemma Rose. Of course, Owen has since returned to England to play for Newcastle.

Jamie and Louise Redknapp
Ex-Spurs star Jamie and singer Louise are only seen out walking their son, Charlie, around the shops. The child is something of a miracle as the proud couple had been trying for four years to conceive; the singer suffers from endometriosis, a condition that makes pregnancy difficult.

Sven-Goran Eriksson and Nancy Dell'Olio
England coach Sven and partner Nancy Dell'Olio – is it on or is it off? According to ex-FA secretary Faria Alam, Sven had been in hot pursuit of her, insisting that his long-term relationship with Nancy was on the rocks.

Thierry Henry and Nicole Merry
Croydon-born model Nicole Merry met Arsenal striker Thierry Henry while filming the Renault Clio adverts. There was plenty of 'va va voom' between the two, because shortly after meeting they started dating, and were married in 2003.

Sol Campbell and Kelly Hoppen
Sol Campbell is the England defender whose goal was disallowed in the Euro 2004 match against Portugal. Kelly is a well-known interiors guru, stepmother to Sienna Miller and 15 years Sol's senior, at 44. The couple have enjoyed an on-off relationship for a couple of years, although Sol has also been linked to tennis star Martina Hingis and singer Dido. He was also at the centre of tabloid allegations that he'd fathered a love-child with ex-girlfriend Janet Taylor.

David James and Amanda Salmon
England goalie David James left his wife of nearly 12 years, Tanya, for his childhood sweetheart, Amanda Salmon in 2003. David walked out on his marriage after *The Sunday People* revealed that they had rekindled their romance via the Friends Reunited website. Amanda also left her partner, but the relationship did not last.

INTERNATIONAL FOOTBALLER'S WIVES AND GIRLFRIENDS

Helene Svedin – Luis Figo

Linda Evangelista – Fabien Barthez

Sheree Murphy – Harry Kewell

Milene Domingues – Ronaldo

Susana Werner – Ronaldo (again!)

Adriana Sklenarikova – Christian Karembeu

Magdalena Hedman – Magnus Hedman

DAVID BECKHAM'S INCREDIBLE FENG SHOE-I

In 2004, David Beckham surprised sports shoe makers Adidas with his sudden interest in Eastern mysticism. While in the design stages of a Beckham signature Predator Pulse boot, the footballer requested that the boffins incorporate the principles of the Chinese art of Feng Shui in a bid to boost its performance. Feng Shui is study of how the positioning and physical characteristics of an object affect the fortunes of its owner.

'I'm very proud to wear these boots because they represent the idea of yin and yang,' said the Real Madrid star of the new cleats. The boot colours represent power and stimulation (red) and class and purity (silver).

Only 723 pairs of the boots were made because 723 is Beckham's combined squad numbers from Manchester United and Real Madrid. Feng Shui experts ordered Beckham to keep and wear pairs number one, seven, 23 and 723. The rest, all size 9 (7+2), were sold to increase good karma and, let's face it, Adidas' profits at nearly $1,000 a pair.

THE 'OUTING' OF GRAHAM LE SAUX

Statistically one in 10 men in the UK is gay. This figure holds true everywhere in the country except in the football changing rooms. There, no one is gay. Football, it seems, remains way too macho and working class to examine its sexuality.

Chelsea defender Graham Le Saux enjoyed a distinguished career at Stamford Bridge and won 36 caps for England, however much of his professional career was marred by repeated claims that he was gay; leading to endless taunts of 'faggot' from crowds as well as, somewhat shockingly, his fellow footballers.

Le Saux is no homophobe and he's clearly not gay either. He has a wife and children. But even this normally even tempered man found the rumours and the taunting drove him bonkers.

How did the rumour start? The view of him on the terraces and in the dressing room was apparently based on the fact he had two A-levels, went away on a camping holiday as a teenager with a male friend, collected antiques and read *The Guardian*. In many other walks of life, this would not be at all unusual, but in soccer, straying from the stereotype of being a hard-drinking, inarticulate, womaniser with a sports car and a silly haircut is apparently to cast serious doubts on your sexuality. Young footballers, gay or not, should take note.

> **I definitely want him to be christened, but I don't know into what religion yet.**
>
> David Beckham, talking about his son, Brooklyn

Posh 'n' Becks are the probably the most famous footballing husband and wife team. A couple whose connections and world beating achievements in football and music have made them recognisable to people of all ages all over the world and a powerful brand for advertisers. But before Posh 'n' Becks were even born, there was another couple whose union made them the most glamourous celebrity couple in the world – Bobby and Tina.

Tina? Yes, Tina Moore was the first high-profile footballer's wife. She was married to her childhood sweetheart, the England captain Bobby Moore, who she met aged just 17. When Moore raised the Jules Rimet trophy after winning the 1966 World Cup in London, the profile of football in the English-speaking world went through the roof as did the fame of Tina and her husband.

They were 'the' couple to have at your bash in Swinging Sixties London. Meanwhile Tina did not stand idle, she used her profile to promote women's charities and sports. Moreover she stood by her husband through the many ups and downs of their life together. Although Tina and Bobby finally split in 1986, they remained close. Tina now lives in Miami and London and has published a biography of her husband and their life together in time for the 40th anniversary of the 1966 World Cup.

Tina Moore – a true original.

I'm an emotional person and I enjoy crying. You know the film *Beaches* with Bette Midler and Barbara Hershey? Sometimes, when I want a good cry I put it on.
Ian Wright

> **I hate to admit this but I don't even know how to
> make a cup of tea or coffee. I can boil a kettle for a
> pot noodle and I've been known to warm up some
> food in the microwave.**
>
> Michael Owen

FOOTBALL 365'S LADIES' CHOICE OF BEST LOOKING FOOTBALLERS OF THE LAST FOUR DECADES

Irreverent football fan site Football 365 conducts an unofficial investigation into the age old question. The pollsters? Twelve Northern women who minds have be sharpened by unlimited alcohol.

1970s – Frank Worthington
'A proper bloke... wouldn't nick your moisturiser...'

1980's – Ricky Villa

'An Argentine version of Frank Worthington and had a massive beard.'

1990's – Eric Cantona,
'He had that rock 'n' roll thing.'

However most hotly disputed was the best looking footballer of today:

Rio Ferdinand 'Too pretty and seriously daft lips.'
David Beckham – 'Loves himself too much and has crap tattoos.'
Ryan Giggs – 'Too much of the gorilla about him.'
Thierry Henry – 'Looks like he should be in a Calvin Klein ad.'
Freddie Ljungberg – 'Looks like he runs a hairdressers.'
Wayne Rooney – 'Argh!'

The winner? A draw between:

Ashey Cole and Alan smith

REAL FOOTBALLERS' WIVES SPEAK OUT AGAINST FOOTBALLERS' WIVES

In April 2004, *The Wimslow Express* ran an interview with three real-life footballers' wives living in Wilmslow, Cheshire who had taken umbrage at the hedonistic lifestyles of the characters portrayed on *Footballers' Wives*, the TV show.

Dawn Ward (wife of Sheffield United's Ashley Ward), Faye Campbell (wife of Everton's Kevin Campbell) and Gemma Curtis (wife of Blackburn's John Curtis of Blackburn) claimed their lives were 'far removed' from the antics of characters Amber and Tanya on TV. And that they were 'shocked – albeit amused – at the tales of lurid sex and bitter rivalry as seen in the series.'

Dawn is a: 'busy mother of two who helps run a nursing home which the couple own as well as keeping a close eye on the designer boutique, Apparel, which she set up in Wilmslow.'

Cynics would point out that the clothes on sale in the shop – exactly the type of high-fashion worn by the characters in the TV series – the real-life footballers' wives do use their connections to raise funds for charity as well. Dawn, Faye and Gemma were models for the day at a catwalk show held to raise cash for Francis House Children's Hospice. They shared the catwalk with professionals from the Boss model agency.

The event raised a fantastic £15,000 proving that the real world of footballers' wives is a little more charitable and less money obsessed than the TV would have us believe.

> I always used to go for blondes and quiet girls, but Victoria is the total opposite – dark and loud.
>
> **David Beckham**

FOOTBALL WITH EVERYTHING –
A SELECTION OF STUPID MERCHANDISE

Chelsea – Monogrammed ladies garter, three pack of thongs.

Newcastle United – Baby soothers (dummies)

Aston Villa – China thimble and bell set

Fulham – Beach inflatable of club badge

Middlesbrough – Dog harness

Southampton – Car mat

Portsmouth – Commemorative stamp

Blackburn – Egg cup set

Tottenham – Leather bound encyclopaedia

Wolves – Commemorative brick (from stands at Molineux)

THE COUPLE THAT PLAYS TOGETHER STAYS TOGETHER

Slovakian supermodel Adriana Sklenarikova is best known for two things. Her modelling for Wonderbra and her marriage to former Real Madrid soccer star Christian Karembeu.

Shortly after their wedding, the new Mrs Karembeu told journalists that she loved her new husband's tough and rugged image. She also claimed that she loved playing soccer with him. How romantic you might say. And it was, until he nearly broke her leg with a slide tackle during a friendly match in their back garden.

'We were playing in the garden in the freezing rain and mud,' she recalled, 'and he did this really hard slide tackle on me and nearly broke my leg. Honestly, it hurt so much.' They both wisely suggested that forthwith her husband only play soccer with his friends. However in the spirit of the marriage, the two of them switched to another sport they could enjoy together. The logic of the proposed alternative was dubious but, nonetheless, they settled on boxing.

The result? Christian promptly broke Adriana's finger.

Fallen heroes

BAD BOYS INC.

GREAT FOOTBALL FIGHTS

1. John Hartson v Eyal Berkovic
West Ham striker Hartson was caught on camera kicking
Berkovic in the head during a training ground brawl.

2. Graham Le Saux v David Batty
The pair squared up during an ill fated Champion Leagues game
in Moscow. The team lost 3-0 to Spartak in 1995.

3. Teddy Sheringham v Andy Cole
Refused to speak to each other at Manchester United after Sheringham
blamed Cole for a goal conceded in a 1998 match against Bolton.

4. Robbie Fowler v Neil Ruddock
The two had a run in on a flight back from a 1995 UEFA cup match in
Moscow. Ruddock blamed Fowler for messing up his designer shoes.

5 Fabrizio Ravenelli v Neil Cox
The Middlesborough two scuffled outside their hotel in the
eve of the 1997 FA Cup final after Ravenelli heard Cox had disputed
his place in the starting line up.

6. Bruce Grobbelaar v Steve McManaman
Came to blows in the penalty area during Liverpool's 1993
defeat by Everton.

7 Graham Hogg v Craig Levein
It kicked off for no specific reason as Hearts played a
1994 pre-season friendly with Raith. Levein broke Hogg's nose.

8. Dean Keily v Andy Todd
Todd thumped keeper Keily during routine training at Charlton.

9. Alan Shearer v Keith Gillespie
A drunken Gillespie threw a punch at Shearer after a night out during a
club break in Dublin. Gillespie missed and Shearer decked him.

10. Mike Flanagan v Derek Hales
Both Charlton players got sent off for fighting
in a third round cup tie in 1979.

FOG ON THE TYNE. HOW PAUL GASCOIGNE WAS LOST

Paul Gascoigne, affectionately known to football crowds as 'Gazza', was the clown prince of English football in the 1990s. His flair and talent as a midfielder combined with his emotional devotion to the game and his great sense of fun, made him a firm favourite on the terraces. But the pressures of fame, commercial commitments and his home life would prove overwhelming.

Paul Gascoigne was born in Gateshead, England on 27 May 1967. He signed for Newcastle United in 1983 as an apprentice and made his first team debut in 1985. In total, he made 99 appearances and scored 25 goals for Newcastle before being bought by Tottenham Hotspur in 1988 for £2 million.

The defining moment of his career came in a white England shirt. After an emotional performance at Italia 90, he cried on the pitch in the semi final after receiving a booking, which would have seen him suspended for the final had England won. The event showed both Gascoigne's fragility and his whole-hearted commitment to the sport and the nation loved him for it. That year he was voted the BBC Sports Personality of the Year.

During Euro 96, Gascoigne was on arguably the best form of his life, scoring a spectacular goal against Scotland. But from then on, it was all downhill. He suffered problems with form, injury and discipline as he spent more time at celebrity parties than he did at the training ground.

France 98 saw him omitted from the England squad for the first time. He had now joined Middlesbrough but continuing problems with drink led to him being released from his contract. After completing rehab for his alcoholism, he drifted from club to club, finally ending up with a trial for the US club DC United. Later, he played for a second division team in China, with the catchy name of 'The Gansu Agricultural Land Reclamation Flying Horses'. It was a long way to fall for a player who had been a household name in the UK. He coped badly, becoming estranged from the football fraternity, which had offered him a means of support, as well as from his wife Sheryl and son amid accusations of domestic violence. However in recent years, he has returned to the game via coaching. True football fans will wish this unique talent and personality all the best as he tackles his demons.

football heroes

YES, YOUR MAJESTY — WEIRD CONTRACT
CLAUSES OF STAR PLAYERS

Edmundo
Contact with Fiorentinea allowed him to go to Rio Carnival. He also got a Cherokee Jeep (which he crashed) and looked at 100 houses before settling on a castle.

Jürgen Klinsmann
His Tottenham contract included a 'happy' clause which meant if he was ever dropped from a game he could quit the club.

Stefan Schwarz
Had booked to go on first passenger flight to the moon. Sunderland manager Peter Reid told him to drop the idea or leave the club.

Attilio Lombardo
In his Crystal Palace contract he demanded a Surrey mansion with a butler and a maid. The club told him to forget it.

Ian Wright
His contract with Arsenal banned him from riding his Harley Davidson motorcycle.

Fabrizio Ravanelli Moveto
His negotiations with Everton broke down after he demanded 28 free first class flight to Italy, along with his £200,000 signing on fee.

Andy Goram
Rangers banned him from representing Scotland at cricket in the summer in case he damaged his hands.

Carlos
Refused to discuss new contract with Real Mallorca because he was convinced that the World would end at the Millennium.

Of the nine red cards this season we probably deserved half of them.

Arsene Wenger

> I spent a lot of money on booze, birds and fast cars.
> The rest I just squandered.
>
> ## George Best

EASY BOY. THE FASTEST SENDING OFFS ON A DEBUT

Being sent off is shameful for any player. Not only does he blot his own copy book but he leaves his teammates to play on with just 10 men and, depending on the tournament, he can be suspended for forthcoming matches. Well, how about doing that on your club debut? Seems unlikely, but in the rush to prove your worth it does happen.

While some players, like Gary Lineker, are never sent off in their career, others, like Vinnie Jones, collect bookings like Clubcard points. Here we celebrate not those who have disgraced themselves the most but those who have been sent for an early bath the fastest in their very first professional game.

When Garry Flitcroft made his debut for Blackburn against Everton in March 1996, he also made the referee's notebook. He was dismissed for elbowing Tony Grant an impressive three minutes after taking to the field. But that's not the record.

In his debut for Burnely, Ade Akinbiyi excelled himself by head butting Sunderland's George McCartney two minutes after coming off the bench. But, even that is not the record.

In October 1997, a young Jason Crowe came on as a substitute in extra time of Arsenal's League Cup clash against Birmingham. No doubt eager to make his mark, he was immediately adjudged to have committed a high tackle. Despite the tender years of the player, referee Uriah Rennie brought out the red card and Crowe's game was over. He'd been on the pitch for 33 seconds. He probably didn't even need to shower afterwards.

football heroes

'When you put yourself in the firing line, you are open to attack,' said Justin Fashanu in an interview in the 1980s. 'I know I'm there to be shot down in flames.' His words would prove eerily prophetic.

Justin and his brother John, who later became captain of Wimbledon FC, both showed huge early talent. At 17, Justin represented Britain on the junior team. At 19, as a centre forward for Norwich City, he scored a goal that's been voted one of the best in history – a magnificent long-range shot from far outside the penalty box. In 1980, he was the first black player purchased for £1 million when he transferred to Nottingham Forest.

It was at Forest that his troubles began. He locked horns with the belligerent manager Brian Clough. Clough disliked the new signing and found it difficult to accept him as 'one of us'. When rumours of Fashanu's homosexuality reached him, Clough suspended and finally sacked him, later calling him 'a bloody poof'.

After Forest, he wandered from team to team. As his career deteriorated, Fashanu was getting headlines again for all the wrong reasons. In 1990, he was the first soccer player to come out publicly. He claimed to have had sex with fellow players and a Member of Parliament. Initially, it looked like a courageous move, but when Fashanu later admitted he'd given interviews for money and that the stories of Westminster seductions were untrue, public opinion turned against him.

Further revelations in 1994 led to his dismissal by Aberdeen for 'conduct unbecoming a professional footballer' in a match against Liverpool. His position in the UK was impossible and he moved to America. However, trouble was never far away. In April 1998, a story broke in the British press that a teenage boy in Maryland, USA had claimed Fashanu had sexually molested him. Fashanu dismissed the accusation as blackmail. It was the final straw. Riddled by paranoia and depression, he hung himself in an East London garage.

Whatever happened, the pressure proved too much for Fashanu. A promising career had gone drastically wrong, in part because his personal life was so at odds with the sport he loved.

SHILT LETS IT ALL GO TO HIS HEAD

Peter Shilton a footballing sinner? Surely not. But maybe he was guilty of pride. After all, he was a man who sometimes let in soft goals because he was always trying to make the perfect save.

In the late 1970s Nottingham Forest had the Indian sign on Liverpool, knocking them out of the European Cup and beating them in the League Cup final. But the FA Cup was never going to be Brian Clough's as Peter Shilton proved at home against Liverpool in the fourth round of the 1979-80 season. Shilton dropped a simple high ball allowing Kenny Dalgleish to score the opening goal in a 2-0 victory. The season before Shilton let Yasuhiko Okudera's weak ground shot slip through his hands for Cologne to equalise in the European Cup semi-finals.

Shilton's pride cost him internationally too. He admitted trying to make too good a save against Poland at Wembley costing England a place in the 1974 World Cup finals, when he failed to hold on to a simple low shot. It was a trait which stayed with the Shilton right up to his 125th and final international game when he lost concentration on the line in the third place play-off of Italia 90 and allowed Roberto Baggio to set up the first goal in England's 2-1 defeat.

VINNIE GOES TO HOLLYWOOD

Despite having retired and taken up a new career as a Hollywood actor, Vinnie Jones has lost none of his bad boy attitude. As a professional Jones was sent off nearly a dozen times in his professional career, and was once shown the yellow card just three seconds into a game. For many the enduring image of Jones on the pitch is the photograph of him crushing the testicles of a young Paul Gascoigne while out of the referee's eyesight.

One day in 2002, Jones was appearing in a friendly soccer match in Hollywood. Fans reported: 'Vinnie sprinted on to the pitch like a greyhound, but was obviously a bit too enthusiastic.' Enthusiastic indeed. Just 15 seconds after coming on as a substitute for a celebrity team, Hollywood United, he launched into one of the opposing team's players, who went down like a sack of potatoes. Jones was, as usual, shown a red card and took an early shower.

IS YOU CAN'T DO THE TIME, DON'T DO THE CRIME –
10 PLAYERS WHO WERE SUSPENSED FOR THEIR ACTIONS.

Willie Woodburn (Rangers, 1954)
Crime: Retaliation after being sent off three times for retaliation
Time: Lifetime ban

Billy McLafferty (Stenhousemuir, 1992)
Crime: Failing to turn up at Scottish FA hearing
Time: Eight and a half months and a £250 fine

Eric Cantona
(Manchester United, 1995)
Crime: Attacking a spectator
Time: Eight months and £10,000 fine

Rio Ferdinand
(Manchester United, 2003)
Crime: Failing to turn up for a drugs test
Time: Eight months

Duncan Ferguson
(Everton, 1995)
Crime: Violent conduct
Time: Twelve matches

Paulo Di Caneo
(Sheffield Wednesday, 1998)
Crime: Shoving a referee
Time: Eleven matches plus three matches for being sent off

Paul Davis (Arsenal, 1988)
Crime: Broke the jaw of Glenn Cockerill
Time: Nine matches and £3,000

Frank Sinclair (Chelsea, West Bromwich, 1992)
Crime: Assaulting a referee
Time: Nine match ban and £600 fine

Patrick Viera (Arsenal, 1999)
Crime: Spitting at Neil Ruddock
Time: Six match ban and £45,000 fine

Roy Keane (Manchester United, 2002)
Crime: Claimed in his autobiography that he had deliberately set out to hurt Alf Inge Haaland
Time: Five match ban and £150,000 fine.

We pulled the self destruct button.
Colin Lee

PLAYERS BEHIND BARS

You could almost put together a lags eleven from the football players who've spent time behind bars. Two things unite these jailbirds in club shirts: talent and a dangerous love of booze.

Not that hot-headed England international Dennis Wise needed much encouragement. Having been sent off three times in the 1998-1999 season, he rounded that year off by receiving a three-month suspended jail sentence for attacking a 65-year-old cab driver outside Terry Venables' exclusive nightclub, Scribes.

Booze and cars played their part in the downfall of Arsenal captain Tony Adams (imprisoned for two months in 1990 for drunk driving into a wall at 70 mph) and George Best, who failed to appear in court for his drink drive charge resulting in an epic drunken chase across London between the wily Best and 20 cops.

But there crimes fade into insignificance compared to former Arsenal and England player, Peter Storey. After retiring Storey dove head first into the criminal life. He started in 1977 by failing to stop at a crossing and headbutting a lollipop man who remonstrated with him. In 1978 he took it up a notch by financing a plan to counterfeit gold coins.

In 1979 he was convicted of living off immoral earnings and running a brothel and even while inside in 1982 he was convicted of stealing two cars back in 1978.

Despite attempting to go straight on his release by running a market stall, he was back in the dock again for assault on an traffic warden and latterly, for smuggling pornographic videos into Britain. As the magistrate sentenced him, she concluded with the words, 'You already know what prisons are like, Mr Storey.'

It's a phrase that suits many a football player.

MARADONA FAILS TO KEEP HIS NOSE CLEAN

The nosedive (forgive the pun) taken in the personal life and professional career of Diego Maradona is one of the most dramatic tales in football. He rose from poverty in his native Argentina to become the most celebrated player of the modern era; second in reputation only to the mighty Pelé. His talent earned him a fortune, a World Cup and the adoration of fans all around the world. But his dark side found him involved with drugs, binge eating and organised crime.

The world caught its first glimpse of Maradona at the World Cup in 1982. Soon after he joined FC Barcelona and later Napoli, where his skill led the team into its most successful era. They won the Italian Championship twice, a Coppa Italia and the UEFA Cup.

By 1986 Maradona was unstoppable, leading the Argentine national team to victory in the World Cup, and scoring two infamous goals against England in the process. But soon the tide began to turn. His love affair with Italian football went sour at the 1990 World Cup in Italy. The Italian fans felt Maradona had

betrayed them when a Maradona-led Argentina defeated the hosts on penalties in front of the home crowd in his adopted city of Naples. The following spring, a dope test showed cocaine traces in his bloodstream. He was banned from Italian and then world football for 15 months.

Bloated, unfit and unrepentant, he returned to Argentina and was promptly arrested for cocaine possession. Released on probation, he sought to revive his playing career in Spain but lasted only half a season. In 1994, a return to the World Cup stage in the US ended abruptly after random dope test found a cocktail of illegal drugs. He finally retired from football on his 37th birthday.

Since the 1990s, Maradona has been battling a cocaine addiction and the chaos of his life. In April, 2004, he suffered a major heart attack following a cocaine overdose and was admitted to intensive care. Although now a bloated version of his former self, his football brilliance and the legacy he left cannot be denied. Indeed an online FIFA poll spoke volumes when it voted him simply, the greatest footballer of the century.

PLAYERS WHO FAILED DRUG TESTS

Rio Ferdinand – Manchester United
2003 'Failed' to turn up for a routine drugs test *Suspended eight months*

Billy Kenny – Everton
1994 Failed clubs own drug test twice *End of contract*

Paul Merson – Arsenal
1994 Admitted to cocaine and alcohol abuse *Three months in rehab*

Craig Whitington – Hudersfield
1996 First British player to test positive for cannabis twice *Sacked by club*

Lee Bowyer – Charlton
1995 Tested positive for cannabis *Suspended*

Chris Armstrong – Crystal Palace
1995 Tested positive for cannabis *Left out of squad on FA advice*

Frank de Boer
Tested postive for Nandrolone *One-year ban reduced to three months*

Roger Stanislaus – Leyton Orient
1996 Found using cocaine *Banned for one year and subsequently sacked*

Jamie Stuart – Charlton
1997 Tested positive for cannabis and cocaine *Sacked by club*

Mark Bosnich – Chelsea
2003 Tested positive for cocaine *Suspended for nine months*

> **I've had 14 bookings this season – eight of which were my fault, but seven of which were disputable.**
> ## Paul Gascoigne

David Beckham as a fallen hero? Nowadays such a statement seems crazy. David Beckham OBE is the highest-paid footballer in Europe, captain of the English national team and an international symbol of fame, glamour and success. But in June 1998, David Beckham was the most hated man in the country. His ejection from a second round World Cup match against Argentina was seen to have led directly to the team's elimination from the tournament. Beckham was mauled by the tabloids, burned in effigy outside an English pub and received death threats. He had let his country down against a hatred rival and humiliated himself on the biggest footballing stage in the world.

Beckham was just 17 when he made his first-team debut. During his first full Premiership season in 1995-1996, Beckham scored eight goals as an unusually young United team went on to win the Premiership and FA Cup double.

Beckham became a household name in his own right the following season after scoring an incredible goal from the half-way line against Wimbledon. He went on to establish himself as an attacking midfielder with his exemplary crossing and goals from free kicks. Beckham went on to play 394 games for Manchester, scoring 85 goals and winning nine medals.

Nationally Beckham had won England caps at both under-21 and youth level, winning his first senior cap against Moldova on 1 September 1996. But nothing could prepare him for the 1998 World Cup in France. Beckham was the only player to make the starting line up in every qualifying game of the finals. However he was left out of the first games of the tournament and so set out to prove himself in the final two games of the group. Against Columbia, he scored one of his now famous free-kicks. In the next game, a second round knock-out match against Argentina, things went disastrously wrong. Having been tackled from behind by the Argentine midfielder Diego Simeone, Beckham went down. Lying on the ground, he impulsively kicked out at Simeone in retaliation catching the Argentinean on the back of the legs. The referee responded with the red card and Beckham suffered the first sending-off of his professional career. The football pundits, Fleet Street and almost the entire country blamed Beckham for England being knocked out that year. Beckham went from being a talented bright hope to public enemy number one.

International heroes

heroes

TALENT FROM ACROSS THE WATER

FIFA WORLD PLAYER OF THE YEAR

2004 **Ronaldinho** (FC Barcelona) *Brazil*

2003 **Zinedine Zidane** (Real Madrid) *France*

2002 **Ronaldo** (Real Madrid) *Brazil*

2001 **Luis Figo** (Real Madrid) *Portugal*

2000 **Zinedine Zidane** (Real Madrid) *France*

1999 **Rivaldo** (Barcelona) *Brazil*

1998 **Zinedine Zidane** (Juventus) *France*

1997 **Ronaldo** (Inter Milan) *Brazil*

1996 **Ronaldo** (Barcelona) *Brazil*

1995 **George Weah** (AC Milan) *Liberia*

1994 **Romario** (Barcelona) *Brazil*

1993 **Roberto Baggio** (Juventus) *Italy*

1992 **Marco Van Basten** (AC Milan) *Holland*

1991 **Lothar Matthaus** (Inter Milan) *Germany*

PETIT'S LUCK

1998 was a rough year for Emmanual Petit. The midfielder scored the final and deciding goal in the 1998 World Cup in France. It took his team and his country to an improbable 3-0 victory over the perennial World Cup favourites, Brazil, and sent the host nation wild. But that wasn't all. Petit's club team Arsenal had, just weeks before the Brazil game, won both the English championship and the FA Cup.

Let me also remind you that Petit himself is no bespeckled nerd. He is tall, blond, muscular and pony-tailed with raffish gallic good-looks and a beautiful former model for a wife.

How could Petit top such achievements? A few days after parading through the streets of Paris on an open-topped bus in front of hundreds of thousands of his adoring countrymen, he wandered casually into a casino and won more than twenty thousand dollars on a one-armed bandit. It was a very good year.

WHOSE SIDE ARE YOU ON? – CHANGING NATIONALITIES

Strange though it may seem, many players have a serious choice to make when it comes to deciding which country they will represent. Boundaries and national rules change and people reach back through their genealogies to find qualifying relatives. Ryan Giggs, for example, played for, and was captain of, the England schoolboy team but, as an adult, he chose to play for Wales.

Sometimes geography can influence the decision. Alfredo di Stefano was born in Buenos Aires in 1926 and played seven times for Argentina as a young man. Due to a player strike in his homeland he moved to Columbia, where big bucks were paid to those who took part in their own (non FIFA) league. There he played for Columbia. Finally he emigrated, signed to Real Madrid, and went on to play for Spain 31 times. Likewise Ladislao Kubala made his debut for Czechoslovakia aged 19. After six games he switched to Hungary. He then emigrated to Barcelona and finally picked up 19 caps for Spain.

Weirdly football officialdom meant that the great Bobby Moore lifted the World Cup as captain of England in 1966 yet later skippered Team America against England as part of a Bicentennial Cup tournament in 1976. He was playing in America for the San Antonio Stars at the time.

Finally how is this for irony? When Welshman Ivor Powell was injured in a war-time clash with England at Wembley, his injury left Wales a man down due to a war-time shortage of players. The English sportingly allowed them to borrow guess who? Former Wales player turned English cap, Stan Mortensen, who had debuted for Wales, but then picked up 23 England caps in his career.

I couldn't settle in Italy – it was like living in a foreign country.
Ian Rush

football heroes

FIVE FOOTBALL PLAYERS WHO HAVE RECEIVED KNIGHTHOODS

1. Sir Trevor Brooking

2. Sir Bobby Charlton

3. Sir Tom Finney

4. Sir Geoff Hurst

5. Sir Matt Busby

SIZE ISN'T EVERYTHING — THE SIZE OF MAJOR TROPHIES

1 FA Premier League Trophy
105.5cm (3ft 5.5in), 25kg (55lb)

2 Intercontinental Cup
78cm (2ft 7in), 29kg (63lb 13oz)

3. UEFA Champions League
74cm (2ft 5in), 8kg (17lb 10oz)

4. UEFA Cup
65cm (2ft 2in), 15kg (33lb)

5 UEFA Cup Winners Cup
60cm (24in), 14kg (30lb 13oz)

6 European Football Championships
50.5cm (20in), 10 kg (22lb)

7. FA Cup
48cm (19in), 5kg (175oz)

8. UEFA Super Cup
42.5cm (17in), 5kg (11lb)

9. FIFA World Cup
36cm (14in), 5kg (11lb), 18 carat gold

10. Carling Cup
27cm (11in), 3kg (105oz)

11. UEFA Intertoto Cup
20cm (8in), 1kg (2lb 3oz)

> **I can't even spell spaghetti never mind talk Italian. How could I tell an Italian to get the ball? He might grab mine.**
>
> Brian Clough, on the influx of foreign players

HIGHEST EARNING SOCCER PLAYERS IN EUROPE

1. David Beckham (Real Madrid) – **25 million euros**
Salary: 6.4 million euros
Bonuses: 200,000 euros
Advertising and commercial revenue: 18.4 million euros in advertising.

2. Ronaldo (Real Madrid) – **19.6 million euros**
Salary: 6.4 million euros
Bonuses: 200,000 euros
Advertising and commercial revenue: 13 million euros in advertising.

3. Zinedine Zidane (Real Madrid) – **13 million euros**
Salary: 6.4 million euros
Bonuses: 200,000 euros
Advertising and commercial revenue: 6.4 million euros in advertising.

4. Christian Vieri (Inter Milan) – **12 million euros**

5. Alessandro Del Piero (Juventus) – **9.5 million euros**

6. Frank Lampard (Chelsea) – **9.4 million euros**
(Source: France Football)

International football is one clog further up the football ladder.
Glenn Hoddle

THE ORIGINS OF GENIUS: PELÉ

'Heroes walk alone, but they become myths when they ennoble the lives and touch the hearts of all of us,' said former US Secretary of State Henry Kissinger. 'For those who love soccer, Edson Arantes do Nascimento, generally known as Pelé, is a hero.'

In the 1960s and 1970s, Pelé travelled the world with his club team Santos and his national team, Brazil, entertaining crowds with his magical brand of soccer. He scored 1,281 goals in his 22-year career.

In Nigeria, a two-day truce was declared in the war with Biafra so that both sides could see him play. The Shah of Iran waited three hours at an airport just to speak with him. A survey in the early 1970s showed that the name Pelé ranked behind Coca-Cola as the most popular brand in Europe.

Nicknamed Dico by his family, he was called Pelé by soccer friends, a word whose origins escape him. It's word that has no meaning in Portuguese and despite Pelé's fears that it was an insult, the name stuck.

Pele was born on 23 October 1940 to Dondinho and Dona Celeste in the impoverished town of Três Corações in south-eastern Brazil. Pele's father was a local professional soccer player who held the distinction of scoring five goals with his head in one game. Eleven-year-old Pelé was shining shoes for a living and playing football for fun with a youth team, when in one of those meetings which can only be predetermined by fate, his skills were noticed by a former World Cup player, Valdemar de Brito.

Four years later, De Brito brought Pelé to the capital Sao Paulo and declared to the disbelieving directors of the professional team in Santos: 'This boy will be the greatest soccer player in the world.'

In his first full season at Santos, he scored 32 goals to top the league's scoring charts. Soon afterward, the 17-year-old was selected for Brazil's 1958 World Cup team and the rest, as they say, is history.

THE FOOTBALL MULTI-MILLIONAIRES

There's a lot of money to be made in football and those and the top certainly have it. Here are those at the very top of the pile in 2004.

1. Roman Abramovich
Chelsea **£7,500m**

2. Joseph Lewis
Tottenham Hotspur/Rangers
£1,800m

3 The Moores family Liverpool
£1,162m

4. Trevor Hemmings
Preston North End
£700m

5. The Walker family
Blackburn Rovers
£650m

6. David Sullivan
Birmingham City
£550m

7. David Gold
Birmingham City **£495m**

8. Mohamed al-Fayed
Fulham **£470m**

9. Harry Dobson
Manchester United
£470m

10. David Murray
Rangers **£450m**

11. Steve Morgan
Liverpool **£320m**

12. David Ross
Leicester City **£312m**

13. John Madejski
Reading **£305m**

14. Dave Whelan
Wigan Athletic
£290m

15. Jack Petchey
Aston Villa/Leeds United
£248m

16. Peter Harrison
Chelsea **£206m**

17. Brian Kennedy
Stockport County
£187m

18. Danny Fiszman
Arsenal **£150m**

19. Sir Jack Hayward
Wolverhampton Wanderers
£150m

20. Stewart Milne
Aberdeen **£132m**
(Source The Sunday Times)

ARMANI OPENS INTERNATIONAL DOORS FOR UK FOOTBALL

Few things are more symbolic of English football's more continental approach than its players' changing attitude to fashion. English football's 'pie and chips' working class image is being replaced with one of sleek internationalism in a national team with a Swedish manager and where many of its key members play their club football abroad.

One sign of this change was when Italian fashion guru Giorgio Armani announced that he would design the new official off-field wardrobe for the England football team.

Journalists were told that the main accent of the range would be on a casual, but elegant look that would consist of a two-button midnight blue wool crepe suit and flat-fronted trousers. Armani also designed accessories such as sunglasses and shoes.

The designer said: 'These young and talented players are positive and relaxed in the way they approach the game, and they play in a modern, fluid way. Sven-Goran Eriksson encourages them to play with flair... they should be dressed in a way that is appropriate to their on-pitch philosophy.'

Indeed, it was Armani who first generated the idea of turning football players into style icons. His 1995 catwalk show featured David James, the Liverpool goalkeeper, who then continued to model Emporio Armani underwear and Armani jeans.

Armani, who has also designed outfits for Chelsea and Newcastle United, is the good friend of many football players like Real Madrid's Ronaldo, Inter Milan's Luis Figo, and Christian Vieri, Juventus' Fabio Cannavaro and AC Milan's Andrei Shevchenko.

'Footballers are today's new style leaders,' he said. 'They have to show an acute combination of mental and physical discipline which makes them genuinely heroic.'

Already used to forking out hundreds of pounds for replica shirts, the fans will be pleased to hear that they can also buy themselves the uniform and accessories in Emporio Armani stores around England in cities like London, Birmingham, Manchester.

FIFA EUROPEAN PLAYER OF THE YEAR

2004 **Andrei Shevchenko** (AC Milan) *Ukraine*
2003 **Pavel Nedved** (Juventus) *Czech Republic*
2002 **Ronaldo** (Real Madrid) *Brazil*
2001 **Michael Owen** (Liverpool FC) *England*
2000 **Luis Figo** (Real Madrid) *Portugal*
1999 **Rivaldo** (Barcelona) *Brazil*
1998 **Zinedine Zidane** (Juventus) *France*
1997 **Ronaldo** (Inter Milan) *Brazil*
1996 **Matthias Sammer** (Borussia Dortmund) *Germany*
1995 **George Weah** (AC Milan) *Liberia*
1994 **Hristo Stoitchkov** (Barcelona) *Bulgaria*
1993 **Roberto Baggio** (Juventus) *Italy*
1992 **Marco Van Basten** (AC Milan) *Holland*
1991 **Jean-Pierre Papin** (Olympic Marseille) *France*
1990 **Lothar Matthaus** (Inter Milan) *Germany*

DAMP SQUIB: BERGKAMP VS ITALY

Dennis Bergkamp finished the 1992-93 season as the top scorer in the Dutch First Division for the third consecutive year. That season one of his four goals for Holland was the clever volleyed lob which helped save a vital World Cup point at Wembley. Then came the inevitable big money call from Italy and Inter Milan. It marks a point in every great player's career when he gets offered his pot of Euro-gold. Sometimes this move is the beginning of greater success and stardom and sometimes, as for our Dennis, it isn't.

The £8 million Inter had paid for him was supposed to help them challenge Milan for the Serie A title. Instead they finished a point above the relegation zone – Bergkamp not only scored a mere eight goals in 30 league matches but five of those were from penalties. His goals in the UEFA Cup were simply not enough of a return against a reported £650,000 a year salary. When his second season didn't improve (this time Inter won nothing), he was sold to Arsenal where he's gone on to fulfil his potential. All this leaves the Italians and Bergkamp himself scratching their heads. Maybe it's something in the water.

YOU WHAT? WEIRD TEUTONIC EXPLANATIONS
AS PENALTIES COME TO EUROPEAN FOOTBALL

West Germany were one of the most successful national teams of the 1970s, beating Holland in the 1974 World Cup final and reaching three European Championship finals in a row. But by 1976 tournament even they were on the wane and probably not the favourites to triumph against Czechoslovakia.

Indeed the Czechs dominated the game going into the break 2-1 ahead. However, West Germany had a sold tradition of recoveries (Hungary in 1954, England in 1970, Holland in 1974). They added to the list here, Bernd Hölzenbein's last-minute header from a corner forcing extra time, which came and went without further goals. Then for first time in a major international final, the game went to penalties.

The first seven went in (Masny, Nehoda, Ondrus, Jurkemik for Czechoslovakia matched by Bonhof, Flohe and Bongartz for West Germany). Then up stepped Uli Hoeness for the German's fourth shot.

Hoeness was no Beckenbauer or even Müller but he was a dynamic blond runner from midfield who had scored twice for Bayern Munich in the 1974 European Cup final. However penalties were not his forte. He even missed one in the 1974 World Cup.

To his credit, he says that he hadn't fancied taking one in this final either but was persuaded by Beckenbauer. It all went pear-shaped.

Later describing the kick, Hoeness said: 'I decided to give him a heavy shot, to try to put it in one corner. The ball was over the wall and I think they found him now a year ago. They had a war and the stadium was destroyed and they found the ball!'

Erm... the translation of that is that he skied it. Over the bar it went and deep into the crowd. Antonin Paneka, finished up with a tight little chip, winning the championship for Czechoslovakia with the last penalty. The ever bizarre Hoeness did not play for West Germany again.

THE PHILOSOPHY OF ERIC CANTONA

Eric Cantona was a French player of immense talent and one for whom the word 'enigma' might have been invented. He played for five teams in France during the late 1980s and early 1990s and during that time established his reputation as brilliant player and a man of fiery, uncompromising temperament. Despite frequent brushes with the French football authorities, he won the French championship with Olympique Marseille and the French Cup with Montpellier. He played too for the French national team then left it calling the coach a 'sac de merde'. Perhaps these views informed his decision no longer pursue his art – and he saw football as an art – in his homeland.

He came to England where he initially joined Leeds, helping them snatch the 1992 League Championship. Then in November 1992 he was transferred for the surprisingly small fee of £1.2 million to Manchester United where he truly came into his own.

Within five years, he took drove United to four League Championships and two FA cups; scoring decisive goals in both finals.

But Cantona remained passionate and uncompromising on and off the pitch. After being sent off during a match against Crystal Palace on 25 January, 1995, Cantona attacked a spectator with a spectacular double-footed karate kick. Cantona claimed the spectator had taunted him with racial abuse. He was promptly banned for nine months.

At a press conference some time later, Cantona explained his actions in a typically esoteric way, to a stunned room of journalists: 'When the seagulls follow the trawler, it is because they think sardines will be thrown into the sea,' he whispered before marching out of the room.

It wasn't until 2003 that Michael Kelly, former head of security at Manchester United, revealed that several people, including Cantona, had prepared the quotation prior to the press conference.

> **I got it from the number 6. I think he was called something-ov.**
> Ronnie Whelan of the Republic of Ireland on swapping shirts
> with a USSR player at Euro '88

> **With the foreign players it's more difficult. Most of them don't even bother with the golf, they don't want to go racing. They don't even drink.**
> Harry Redknapp

TERRIBLE EVENTS AT HEYSEL CHANGE EUROPEAN FOOTBALL FOREVER

The death and disaster on the terraces at the Heysel Stadium in Brussels during the 1985 European Cup Final was a vital wake-up call for English clubs to deal with their trouble-making fans. It led to the physical exlusion of many British fans from Europe and a disgraceful reputation for hooliganism that has haunted us ever since.

Although Liverpool and Juventus vehemently opposed the idea, the Belgium authorities had distastrously decided to allocate a section of the stands to neutral fans. Within minutes of the match starting, Liverpool fans began to attack their counterparts from Juventus leading to the collapse of the retaining wall. They later claimed that rocks and other missiles had been launched by the Juventus fans, leading to retaliation.

In the panic that ensued, many fans were crushed or trampled to death. Of the 39 people who died, 32 were Italians, four were Belgian, two were French and one was Irish.

UEFA banned English clubs from competing in Europe indefinitely. In practice, English clubs returned to Europe in 1990, although it was another season before Liverpool were allowed back in. The Heysel stadium itself has since been completely rebuilt, and is now called the King Baudouin Stadium.

The fans

THE ROAR OF THE CROWD

CELEBRITY FOOTBALL FANS

Arsenal – Martin Kemp, Jeremy Beadle, Clive Anderson
Aston Villa – Iain Duncan Smith, Prince William
Birmingham City – Jasper Carrott
Blackburn Rovers – Jack Straw
Bolton Wanderers – Peter Kay, Vernon Kay
Charlton Athletic – Jim Davidson, Gary Bushell, Michael Grade
Chelsea – Dennis Waterman, Michael Caine
Everton – Tom O'Connor, Freddie Starr
Fulham – Keith Allen, Hugh Grant
Liverpool – Cilla Black, Jimmy Tarbuck
Manchester City – Bernard Manning, Steve Penk
Manchester United – Steve Coogan, Ulrika Jonson, Gary Rhodes
Middlesbrough – Bob Mortimer, Roy 'Chubby' Brown
Newcastle United – Tony Blair, Robson Green
Leeds – Jeremy Paxman
Sunderland – Kate Adie
Tottenham Hotspur – Salmon Rushdie, Jude Law
West Bromwich – Lenny Henry, Cat Deeley
West Ham United – John Cleese, Ray Winstone

DOC'S DIAL-A-CROWD HELPS DEPRESSED FANS

In 2003, Britain psychologist John Castleton, while engaged in a study of football fans, noticed that many of his subjects became depressed at the end of season. So pronounced was the distress some of them felt at being deprived their favourite game, he identified a syndrome that he named 'End of Season Affective Disorder' among soccer fans.

'Football fans clearly hold a deep rooted relationship with their team,' he explained. 'As a result – like any other close bond – to have that central pillar suddenly removed, could cause a quite obvious existential crisis. Often fans will feel a void, an emptiness or loss.'

In an effort to help those suffering from the disorder, Castleton set up a telephone helpline. Fans could call up and listen to goal celebrations and other football-related sounds to ease their anxiety.

FEVER PITCH – NICK HORNBY OUTS THE TRUE FOOTBALL FANS

Strange as it may seem to have an author in a book about football heroes, it's true to say that Nick Hornby, and his book *Fever Pitch*, did a great deal for modern football. The book brought the national game out of the closet and made it okay to support football again. Not just for men but for families and women too.

By the early 1980s, English football had a bad reputation. A decade of hooliganism, international bans and violent outrages had all but banished English fans from Europe and families from the terraces. The media projected an image of football fans as obsessive trouble makers and untamed animals who were now, thanks to new crowd control measures, literally kept in cages at the side of football pitches.

As Nick Hornby wrote in *The Observer*: 'You have to remember that the public perception of football for most of the 1980s was summed up by a *Sunday Times* article which claimed that it was "a slum sport for slum people". I had friends – lawyers, teachers – who would look incredulous when I said I was a football fan. It was like saying you followed wrestling.'

Fever Pitch changed all that. Essentially it was Hornby's autobiography, a familiar tale of a life dedicated to football and Arsenal in particular. Here was a normal, successful and articulate man who loved football with a passion and hated hooliganism. The scales fell from many people's eyes, particularly those in the middle classes who had previously shunned the game.

The book came out in the shadow of the Heysel and Hillsborough disasters and coincided with rise of the New Lads and Ladettes of the *Loaded* generation. These new fans found the grounds clean and safety conscious and many of the rowdier element either weaned out internally or chastened by the tragedies. The result was the game quickly became popular, accessible and even trendy again. Within a few years, fathers were taking their sons to games once more and football was back where it belonged – a family game at the heart of English society.

TOP FOOTBALL CROWD NAMES

Liverpool – The Reds

Chelsea – The Blue and White Army

Red Star Belgrade – The Heroes

Arsenal – The Gooners

West Ham – The Irons

Rangers – The Huns

Manchester United – The Red Army

Everton – The Blues

I've always been a childhood Liverpool fan, even when I was a kid

Harry Kewell

SPORTSMAN FOOTBALL FANS

1. Arsenal – Frankie Dettori, Audley Harrison

2. Aston Villa – Jane Sixsmith

3. Blackburn Rovers – Kenneth Wolstenholme

4. Bolton Wanderers – Steve Ryder

5. Charlton Athletic – Carl Foggerty

6. Chelsea – Lawrence Dallagio, Steve Redgrave

7. Everton – Matt Dawson, John Parrott

8. Liverpool – Viv Richards

9. Manchester United – Mike Atherton, John Virgo

10. Newcastle United – Chris Eubank

11. Sunderland – Steve Cram

12. Tottenham Hotspur – Barry McGuigan

13. West Ham United – Lennox Lewis, Graham Gooch

Football fans will put up with a lot from their heroes. But perhaps the greatest sign of their devotion to those on the pitch is their willingness to put up with their antics off it. There is no greater example of this than their purchasing of footballers' records. We are not talking about inspirational team singalongs for specific tournaments but actual attempts by professional sportsmen to pass themselves off as professional singers.

Gazza's version of 'Fog on the Tyne', performed with Geordie folk rockers Lindisfarne, actually went to number two in the charts thanks to the devotion of his fans. However Kevin Keegan's disco croon, 'Head over Heels in Love', only made it to number 31. Andy Cole's upbeat dance offering, 'Outstanding', failed to trouble the charts.

Terry Venables stuck closer to home with a good old East End stomping version of 'What Do You Want to Make Those Eyes at Me For?'. But again the single was quickly remaindered. Many, many copies of fellow manager Ron Atkinson's Christmas single, 'It's Christmas: Let's give love a try', are presumably available from car boot sales across the country.

Most worryingly a genuine pop career looked in the offing for a duo of terrible mullets, Glenn Hoddle and Chris Waddle, with their 1980s rock ballad, 'Diamond Lights'. Fortunately for everyone involved, they chose not to pursue it.

Finally, it's not just English players who have deluded themselves about their vocal talents. Pray that you never hear Johan Cruyff's Euro offering, the bizarrely titled 'Oei Oei Oei'. That got to number 21. Heaven help us.

> **We're football people, not poets, but obviously I'm disappointed with the result.**
> ## Mick McCarthy

AVERAGE 2004-05 ATTENDANCES OF
CURRENT PREMIERSHIP CLUBS

1. Manchester United **67,748**
2. Newcastle United **51,844**
3. Manchester City, **45,192**
4. Liverpool, **42,587**
5. Chelsea, **41,870**
6. Arsenal, **37,979**
7. Aston Villa, **37,354**
8. Everton, **36,834**
9. Tottenham, **35,926**
10. Middlesbrough, **32,012**
11. Sunderland, **28,821**
12. Birmingham City, **28,760**
13. West Ham, **27,403**
14. Charlton, **26,403**
15. Bolton, **26,006**
16. West Brom, **25,987**
17. Blackburn Rovers, **22,315**
18. Portsmouth, **20,072**
19. Fulham, **19,838**
20. Wigan, **11,563**

A SOCCER RIOT – LIBYAN STYLE

During a soccer game in Tripoli, Libya in 1996, a team sponsored by a son of President Qadhafi suffered a questionable call which started an on pitch brawl. When spectators began jeering the scuffling players, the younger Qadhafi and his bodyguards opened fire on the crowd. Some of the opposing teams fans didn't take this lightly and returned fire, resulting in a death toll claimed to be as high as 50. Afterward, President Qadhafi declared a period of mourning and ordered that all national TV broadcasts of football be transmitted in black and white. A touching gestured rendered largely futile as virtually no one in Libya owned a colour television at the time.

MUSICIANS WHO LOVE FOOTBALL

Arsenal – John Lydon, Dido
Aston Villa – Nigel Kennedy, Ozzy Osbourne
Chelsea – Damon Albarn, Suggs
Everton – Paul McCartney
Liverpool – Mel C, Chris de Burgh
Manchester City – Liam and Noel Gallagher
Manchester United – Ian Brown, Richard Ashcroft
Middlesbrough – Chris Rea
Newcastle United – Sting, Jimmy Nail
Sunderland – Dave Stewart
Tottenham Hotspur – Status Quo, Phil Collins
West Bromwich – Eric Clapton
West Ham United – David Essex

OSAMA BIN LADEN: ARSENAL'S NUMBER ONE FAN

When Arsenal FC lists its high-profile football fans, it probably leaves out its most notorious supporter – the terrorist Osama Bin Laden. Bin Laden picked up his passion for the club while visiting supporters in London in 1994. He went to see Arsenal play four times during this period, even buying his sons gifts from the club's souvenir shop, and later revealed to friends that he was deeply impressed by the passion he saw displayed by the team's fans.

Bin Laden's visits to the terraces were cut short when he was forced to flee the country for Sudan. He would later be linked to a plot to massacre the American and British teams at the 1998 World Cup in France. Indeed according to bin Laden biographer Yossef Bodansky, Al Qaeda bombed the US Embassies in Kenya and Tanzania in August 1998 in part because of 'the failure of the primary operation, an attack on the soccer World Cup'.

He is still remembered at Arsenal, however, in one of their fan's chants: 'He's hiding near Kabul/ He loves the Arsenal/ Osama/ Oh oh oh oh!'

> **It's a game we've got to win.**
> **It's also a game we've not got to lose.**
> ## Graham Taylor

PRICELESS (OR NOT) SILVERWARE FOR SALE IN SOTHEBY'S

What price would you put on a World Cup winners medal? Some might say such a thing is simply priceless, others, namely those who value for major auction houses like Sotheby's and Christie's, could give you a more accurate cash value.

There is a growing market in football memorabilia shirts, medal and trophies have all gone under the hammer courtesy of players looking to raise money for themselves or their favourite charities. Some of these treasures go to private collectors, others back to the clubs themselves if they're making a laudable financial investment in their history. Here are some of the items which have recently gone under the hammer.

Bobby Moore's collection of trophies and medals were bought by West Ham United in June 2000 for £1.8 million. West Ham also paid £158,000 for Geoff Hurst's England World Cup winner's medal.

£274,410 was raised by 129 lots (including a World Cup shirt, cap and man of the match trophy) put up by Geoff Hurst in September 2000.

£157,750 was the price paid by an anonymous bidder for Pelé's famous number 10 shirt from the 1970 World Cup.

£124,750 was paid for Gordon Bank's England World Cup winner's medal by an anonymous bidder.

A selection of material (caps, medals and a blazer) owned by Billy Wright, the first man to get 100 England caps, went for £100,000. Meanwhile, £88,000 would have got you a selection of trophies, caps and medals once owned by Ray Kennedy. Finally, £80,000 was the final bid on a selection of material (trophies, caps, medals) owned by the late, great Sir Alf Ramsey. The objects went into collections at his previous clubs, Tottenham and Ipswich.

It's impossible to write about football fans and not mention the disaster at Hillsborough. It was probably English football's darkest hour, a deadly human crush that occurred on 15 April 1989, at Sheffield's Hillsborough football stadium.

Liverpool were playing in the FA Cup semi-final against Nottingham Forest. Hillsborough, like most stadiums of the time, had placed high spiked fencing between the spectators and the pitch, in an effort to curb the hooliganism which had plagued the sport for years. The terraces were further divided by fencing into 'pens' to aid crowd control.

The game's kick off was scheduled for 3pm but due to a variety of factors, including traffic delays on the route to Sheffield from Liverpool, many Liverpool supporters arrived late. Between 2pm and 2.45pm there was a considerable build up of fans in the small area outside the turnstiles at the Leppings Lane End, full of fans eager to enter the stadium before the match started. A bottleneck soon developed with an estimated 5,000 fans trying to get through the turnstiles. The police decided to open a second set of gates which did not have turnstiles (Gate C). The resulting inpouring of hundreds of fans into the already over-crowded central pens crushed spectators into the fencing.

It was not until 3:06pm that the referee stopped the game. By this time a small gate in the fencing had been opened through which some fans had managed to escape the crush – others climbed over the fencing, and other fans were pulled up by fellow fans into the upper tier above the Leppings Lane End terrace. The pitch quickly started to fill with people sweating and gasping for breath, those with crush injuries, and with the bodies of the dead. The police and ambulance services were overwhelmed by the scale of the disaster and fans helped as best they could, some tearing down advertising hoardings to act as makeshift stretchers.

Hillsborough ultimately took the lives of 96 people, with 766 fans receiving injuries. The horror of the disaster was seen by all as the match was being broadcast on television. It shocked the nation. A permanent tribute to those who lost their lives can be found alongside the Shankly Gates at Anfield. A further tribute was set up in 1999 at Hillsborough.

NICE STAND, SHAME ABOUT THE NAME

Clubs could do well to think twice before naming new parts of their ground. In November 2003, Manchester City were looking forward to the unveiling of a magnificent new stand in their stadium.

Unsure of what to call the construction, the club ran a online poll for fans to decide whether the construction be dedicated to the legacy of their former manager, Joe Mercer, or their legendary midfield player, Colin Bell. As it turned out, the Bell lobby prevailed and the naming was confirmed.

However the announcement sparked an embarrassing public row after it was revealed that the poll, which had been hosted by Manchester City's official website, was alleged to have been hijacked by rival fans. City back-room staff feared that rival fans had voted for Bell ahead of Mercer so that they could dub the stand... the Bell End.

20 PREMIERSHIP CLUB NICKNAMES

1. Arsenal – The Gunners
2. Aston Villa – The Villans
3. Birmingham City – The Blues
4. Blackburn Rovers – The Rovers
5. Bolton Wanderers – The Trotters
6. Charlton Athletic – Addicks
7. Chelsea – The Blues
8. Everton – The Toffees
9. Fulham – The Cottagers
10. Liverpool – The Reds
11. Manchester City– The Citizens
12. Manchester United – The Red Devils
13. Middlesbrough – The Boro
14. Newcastle United – The Magpies
15. Portsmouth – Pompey
16. Sunderland – The Black Cats
17. Tottenham Hotspur – Spurs
18. West Bromwich – The Baggies
19. West Ham United – The Hammers
20. Wigan Athletic – The Latics

Goalkeepers and goal scorers

NOT ALWAYS THE SAFEST HANDS IN SOCCER

JACK OF ALL TRADES — 10 GOALKEEPERS WHO HAVE SCORED GOALS

1. Jimmy Glass (Carlisle United) — Parried header
2. Bruce Grobbelaar (Crewe Alexander) — Spot kick
3. Mart Poom (Sunderland) — Header
4. Paul Robinson (Leeds United) — Last-minute equaliser
5. Brad Friedel (Blackburn Rovers) — From a corner
6. Ray Clemence (Tottenham) — Scored in friendly against Guernsey
7. Peter Schmeichel (Manchester United) — Corner in UEFA Cup tie
8. Peter Shilton (Leicester) — Winner against Southampton
9. Jim Platt (Middlesbrough) — Used as emergency striker
10. Mark Bosnich (Australia) — Penalty spot

I was saying the other day, how often the most vulnerable area for goalies is between their legs...

Andy Gray

THE WISDOM OF DAVID JAMES

Being the goalkeeper for a top-flight team can sometimes be, well, a bit boring. England keeper, David James, once recalled a tale about Liverpool's Bruce Grobbelaar, who had been left with nothing to do thanks to the skill of his teammates: 'Liverpool were six-nil up, and someone handed him an umbrella and he just sat there by the post, out of the rain.'

This story was not the first time James had shown his admiration for things other than keeping goal. During an interview with lad's mag *FHM*, James was asked to comment on a remark by the French writer and fellow goalkeeper, Albert Camus, who once wrote, 'one sentence will suffice for the modern man: He fornicated and read the papers.'

Asked if that comment did not also describe modern football, James replied emphatically: 'No.'

He then elaborated. 'I don't read the paper.'

FIGURES IN THE FOG

Fog has messed up the odd match, as Sam Bartram, the goalkeeper for Charlton Athletic in the 1950s, knew only too well. He was left defending his goal after a heavy fog blighted a league game against Chelsea.

The fog rolled in quickly after kick off covering the whole field, but luckily for Bartram his team were dominating the game and most of action took place at the far end, swathed in fog. He remained on the goal line, trying to keep warm, and listening for any action that was coming his way.

'I paced up and down my goal line, happy in the knowledge that Chelsea were being pinned in their own half,' he recalled later. 'The boys must be giving the Pensioners the hammer, I thought smugly.'

But as time passed he began to get worried. He knew that there had been no score as no players were coming back to line up. He decided to make several advances outside the penalty area, but could see nothing.

A figure at last loomed out of the curtain of fog. It was a policeman! 'What on earth are you doing here?' he asked. 'The game was stopped a quarter of an hour ago. The field's completely empty.'

Bartram reported that when he finally groped his way to the dressing-room, the rest of the Charlton team, already out of the bath, were convulsed with laughter.

> **The goalkeeper is the jewel in the crown and getting at him should be almost impossible. It's the biggest sin in football to make him do any work.**
>
> George Graham

10 NICKNAMES OF UK FOOTBALL PLAYERS

Tony Adams – Donkey

David Beckham – Spice Boy

Stan Collymore – Stan the man

Kenny Dalglish – King Kenny

Paul Gascoigne – Gazza

Ryan Giggs – Welsh Wizard

Mark Hughes – Sparky

Paul Ince – Guv'nor

Teddy Sheringham – Ready Teddy

PENALTY SHOOT OUT RESULTS IN THE EUROPEAN CHAMPIONSHIP

1976 – (F) Czechoslovakia – FR Germany	2-2	5-3	(5 and 4 shots)
1980 – (3/4) Czechoslovakia – Italy	1-1	9-8	(9 shots each)
1984 – (SF) Spain – Denmark	1-1	5-4	(5 shots each)
1992 – (SF) Denmark – Netherlands	2-2	5-4	(5 shots each)
1996 – (QF) England – Spain	0-0	4-2	(4 shots each)
1996 – (QF) France – Netherlands	0-0	5-4	(5 shots each)
1996 – (SF) Czech Rep. – France	0-0	6-5	(6 shots each)
1996 – (SF) Germany – England	1-1	6-5	(6 shots each)
2000 – (SF) Italy – Netherlands	0-0	3-1	(4 shots each)
2004 – (QF) Portugal – England	2-2	6-5	(7 shots each)
2004 – (QF) Netherlands – Sweden	0-0	5-4	(6 shots each)

THE FIX IS IN – BRUCE GROBBELAAR VS. THE SUN

In 1999, former Liverpool stalwart Bruce Grobbelaar found himself defending more than the Anfield goal in the High Court. Instead the South African-born Zimbabwean goalkeeper found himself standing up for the integrity of the entire game against accusations of widespread match fixing. The charges were levelled against him, his fellow Premier League players John Fashanu and Hans Segers and the businessman Heng Suan Lim by *The Sun*.

It was alleged that Grobbelaar took £40,000 to make sure Liverpool lost 3-0 away to Newcastle in 1993. It was also said he had blown his chance of £125,000 more in a 1994 game against Manchester United, which ended in a 3-3 draw, by accidentally making a sensational save in a match he was trying to lose. Included in the case was evidence of attempted match fixing in another five football matches.

The newspaper claimed that Grobbelaar was fixing the matches under the instruction of a shadowy Asian betting ring. It said secretly recorded video tapes it held, one of which showed Grobbelaar

accepting a £2,000 payment, were 'absolutely damning'.

The accusation seemed crazy to Liverpool fans not least as Grobbelaar had enjoyed such an exemplary career. He had joined the club in 1981 from the Vancouver Whitecaps, and played 627 first team games. At Liverpool he was popular with the crowd and became famous for his eccentric and flamboyant style.

When the case was picked up by the police, following up on evidence submitted to them by *The Sun*, Grobbelaar pleaded not guilty, claiming he was only gathering evidence with the intent of taking it to the police himself. After two successive trials, in both of which the jury could not agree on a verdict, he and his co-defendants were cleared in November 1997.

Grobbelaar said after the High Court case: 'This is a day that we can all relish because it ends the slur on football in this country and the game that we love.' But the case was far from over. In August 1999, Grobbelaar sued *The Sun* for libel and asked for substantial damages over the series of articles they had published about him, arguing: 'It was not the money I was after, I was just trying to clear my name in football.' He was awarded £85,000.

Far from clearing his name, his libel victory provoked *The Sun* further. They appealed. The case was eventually taken to the House of Lords in 2001. There they took a rather different view of Grobbelaar's 'innocence'. The Lords slashed his award to just £1, the lowest libel damages possible under English law, and ordered him to pay *The Sun*'s legal costs, estimated at time to be around £500,000. Grobbelaar was

unable to do so and was declared bankrupt.

Despite this verdict being somewhat less than a vote of confidence, Grobbelaar and his legal team continue to maintain his innocence. His solicitor said after the Lords returned their verdict:

'He is one of the greatest goalkeepers ever and well-respected in the profession. He knows that he has never tried to fix a game in his life and he never would.'

Grobbelaar has since moved back to South Africa.

TEN NICKNAMES OF INTERNATIONAL PLAYERS

Roberto Baggio – Golden Ponytail

Dennis Bergkamp – Non-flying Dutchman

Eric Cantona – King Eric

Marcel Desailly – The Rock

Edmundo – Animal

Jürgen Klinsmann – Klinsi

Diego Maradona – Dishevelled One

Ariel Ortega – Little Donkey

Ronaldo – Phenomenon

Christian Vieri – Bobo

THE GREATEST GOALIE WHO EVER LIVED – GORDON BANKS

Born	**30 December 1937 (Sheffield)**

Career	**1955-59:** Chesterfield
	1959-67: Leicester City
	1967-72: Stoke City
	1977-78: Fort Lauderdale Strikers

Honours	**1961:** FA Cup runner-up (Leicester City)
	1963: FA Cup runner-up (Leicester City)
	1964: League Cup (Leicester City)
	1965: League Cup runner-up (Leicester City)
	1972: League Cup (Stoke City)
	1972: Footballer of the Year

England has produced some legendary goalkeepers over the years, but none more so that Gordon Banks. Renowned for his lightning fast reactions, he was a key player in the victorious 1966 World Cup team and made one of the sport's most iconic saves in the subsequent tournament in 1970.

Born in Sheffield, Banks joined third-division team Chesterfield as an apprentice in 1955. He made his debut for the team the following year. Four years and 23 matches later, he left Chesterfield for Leicester City. It was here that he started to show his true potential, reaching the final of the FA Cup in his second season – the first of two FA Cup finals he would manage that decade.

Banks then joined the national side under coach Alf Ramsey. He became the cornerstone of the team for the two World Cups that followed, proving time and time again through his agile saves and athletic prowess why he was England's first choice for goalkeeper.

When England met West Germany in the final of the 1966 World Cup final, it was England who dominated and Banks had little to do as England achieved its historic 4-2 victory. That would not be the case four years later, when England travelled to Mexico to defend its title.

By this time playing for Stoke City — his place at Leicester had been usurped by the young hopeful, Peter Shilton — Banks maintained his England shirt for the 1970 World Cup competition. It was here that he pulled out 'The Save of the Century' in a match against Brazil in the group stages.

Banks was far off his line when Pelé launched an incredible powerhouse header from a Jairzinho cross into the bottom right-hand corner of the goal. Certain of its success, Pelé had begun to celebrate. But as the ball hit the ground in front of the goal, Banks managed to flick it with his outstretched right hand over the bar. Pelé would later describe the save as the greatest he'd ever seen. England nonetheless went on to lose the game 1-0 and later lost to arch rivals West Germany in the quarter finals when Banks was sidelined by illness.

Two years later he would lose the sight in his right eye after a car accident. He now lives in quiet retirement but is still regarded by many as the best goalkeeper England, if not the world, has ever produced.

You can't play with a one armed goalkeeper... not at this level.
Kevin Keegan

PRAYING FOR TIME

The Lord moves in mysterious ways. Or, at least, he does in Brazil. Seconds after the kick-off in a match between Corinthians and Rio Preto at Bahia Stadium in Brazil, Corinthian striker Roberto Rivelino scored a miraculous goal. The goal was the result of a left foot drive from the halfway line after a single pass to open the game.

The ball flew right past Rio Preto goalkeeper Senhor Isadore Irandir and into the back of the net. Why did the keeper miss such a doozy of a shot? He was still kneeling in the goal mouth finishing his pre-match prayers.

THE ART OF KEEPING GOAL

They call football the beautiful game and the world's favourite sport has often found itself a subject for artists. But none as strange as Antonio Becerro. Becerro is the Chilean equivalent of Damien Hirst, who came to fame as the result of a jaw dropping exhibition constructed from embalmed dogs.

For his homage to football, he teamed up with soccer star Francisco Huaiquipan to produce an outstandingly curious art exhibition. It was a painting that was designed to 'evolve' as Huaiquipan took penalty shots, with a freshly painted football, with a huge white canvas which took the place of a goal.

Becerro himself played the role of goalkeeper, dressed from head to foot in white.

TOP GOALSCORERS IN INTERNATIONAL FOOTBALL

1. Ali Daei, Iran (1993-) – 106 goals

2. Ferenc Puskás, Hungary/Spain (1945-56) – 84 goals
Puskás played for Hungary 85 times and Spain on four occasion. He scored all 84 goals while playing for Hungary

3. Pelé, Brazil (1957-71) – 77 goals

4= Sándor Kocsis, Hungary (1948-56) – 75 goals

4= Bashar Abdullah, Kuwait (1996-) – 75 goals

6. Gerd Müller, West Germany (1966-74) – 68 goals

7. Majed Abdullah, Saudi Arabia (1978-94) – 67 goals

8= Hossam Hassan, Egypt (1985-) – 64 goals

8= Kiatisuk Senamuang, Thailand (1993-) – 64 goals

10. Jassem Al-Houwaidi, Kuwait (1992-) – 63 goals

Source: Roberto Mamrud, Karel Stokkermans and RSSSF 1998/2005

football heroes

DAVID ICKE GOES NUTS

David Icke, television sports presenter turned prophet is such a public figure of ridicule and intrigue that it is easy to forget he started life as a goalkeeper.

Born in Leicester, Icke left school to play in goal for Coventry City and Hereford United until crippling arthritis forced him to retire aged 21. He joined a local newspaper in Leicester as a reporter, moving through regional radio and television before joining the BBC as a sports presenter. From there he moved to the Green Party, becoming national media spokesperson.

It was in 1990, that things started to change. He wrote in his online biography (www.davidicke.com) that in March 1990 he received a message from the spirit world through a medium. She told him that he was a healer, 'here to heal the earth', chosen as a youngster for his courage, and charged with communicating the message that will change the world. 'In 20 years there will be a different kind of flying machine, very different from the aircraft of today,' she continued. 'There will be great earthquakes. These will come as a warning to the human race. They will occur in places that have never experienced them. Taking oil from the seabed is destabilising the inner earth. The sea spirits will rise and stop men taking oil. The sea will reclaim the land and humans will see that they cannot do these terrible things. They cannot abuse the elements. They have to be treated with respect.'

Dressed only in turquoise, Icke set out to spread this message, but it was met with derision from all sides. The Green Party banned him from speaking at party public meetings and his announcement that he was 'a son of the Godhead' on a Terry Wogan show in 1991 was met with laughter from the studio audience, derision in the press, and suggestions that he was mentally ill.

After being widely ridiculed, he disappeared from public view for a short time. He now lives in Ryde on the Isle of Wight, where he makes occasional public appearances. He does lecture tours in the US and has written 15 books detailing his radical vision.

SAFE HANDS, DEADLY FEET. KEEPERS HAVE A GO AT GOAL

Goalkeepers are better known for saving goals that scoring them. But despite being some 100-odd yards away from the action, goalkeepers from time-to-time will step up to score vital goals for their sides.

Paraguayan goalie José Luis Chilavert has regularly scored from the penalty spot for both club and country thanks to his mighty right foot. In 1998 he curled a free kick around both a wall and his opposite number during an international against Argentina in Buenos Aires. While in 1999 he became the first goalkeeper to score a hat-trick in the history of the game, while playing for Velez Sarsfield against Ferro Carril Oeste.

There is a history of goalscoring goalkeepers. Prior to 1912, goalkeepers regularly appeared on the score sheet as they were allowed to handle the ball up to the halfway line! It was under these rules that two opposing goalkeepers both scored in the same match (Third Lanark v Motherwell, 1910). The one and only match in which both keepers have scored since, occurred in August 2000 when Velez Sarsfield's Jose Luis Chilavert (who else?) and River Plate's Roberto Bonano both defeated each other from the penalty spot.

Arguably the most famous goal by a keeper in English football was Pat Jennings' effort in the 1967 Charity Shield while playing for Spurs. This goal cannot be credited entirely to skill as Jennings unremarkable clearance was caught by a gust of wind sending the ball right past his opposite number, Alex Stepney of Manchester United. Unfortunately for Stepney, the whole incident was caught for posterity on camera by *Match of the Day*.

That Seaman is a handsome young man but he spends too much time looking in his mirror rather than at the ball. You can't keep goal with hair like that.

Brain Clough, on the pony-tailed former England goalkeeper

TEN GOALKEEPERS WHO HAVE SCORED GOALS FROM GOAL KICKS

1. Chris Mackenzie for Hereford against Bradford's Maik Taylor

2. Iain Hesford for Maidstone against Hereford's Tony Elliot

3. Ray Charles for East Fife against Stranraer's Bernard Duffy

4. Alan Patteron for Glentoran against Linfield's George Dunlop

5. Andy McLean for Cliftonville against Linfield's George Dunlop (again!)

6. Andy Goram for Hibs against Morton's Dave Wylie

7. Steve Ogrizovic for Coventry against Sheffield Wednesday's Martin Hodge

8. Steve Sherwood for Watford against Coventry's Raddy Avramovic

9. Ray Cashley for Bristol City against Hull's Jeff Wealands

10. Peter Shilton for Leicester City against Southampton's Campbell Forsyth.

EVERY CLOUD HAS A SILVER LINING

German goalkeeper Oliver Kahn was dismayed when, during the 2002 World Cup final, he mishandled a shot and allowed Brazil's Ronaldo to tap the ball into the net for the opening goal.

However, far from ruining the Bayern Munich player's career the footballing blooper resulted in a massive cash bonus. His mistake titillated the eccentric Japanese and earned him immense sympathy in the land of the rising sun. Such was his subsequent fame that his value to advertisers skyrocketed and one of then, the tyre giant Bridgestone, promptly signed him to a multi-million dollar advertising deal before the cup had been lifted.

To be fair to Kahn, he'd actually performed rather well in the tournament as a whole and was voted the outstanding player of the World Cup. He's no slouch in the advertising department either, among his other endorsements are Adidas, Lion Bar, Tabac perfume for men, a pay-TV channel (Premiere) and the Japanese financial service provider Tendenz.

World Cup heroes

heroes

TALES FROM THE GREATEST SHOW ON EARTH

WORLD CUP WINNERS

2002 Korea/Japan
Brazil 2-0 Germany
Runners up: Turkey, Korea

1998 France
France 3-0 Brazil
Runners up: Croatia, Holland

1994 USA
Brazil 0-0 Italy (3-2 in penalties)
Runners up: Sweden, Bulgaria

1990 Italy
West Germany 1-0 Argentina
Runners up: Italy, England

1986 Mexico
Argentina 3-2 West Germany
Runners up: France, Belgium

1982 Spain
Italy 3-1 West Germany
Runners up: Poland, France

1978 Argentina
Argentina 3-1 Holland (Extra Time)
Runners up: Brazil, Italy

1974 West Germany
West Germany 2-1 Holland
Runners up: Poland, Brazil

1970 Mexico
Brazil 4-1 Italy

Runners up: West Germany, Uruguay

1966 England
England 4-2 West Germany (ET)
Runners up: Portugal, USSR

1962 Chile
Brazil 3-1 Czechoslovakia
Runners up: Chile, Yugoslavia

1958 Sweden
Brazil 5-2 Sweden
Runners up: France, West Germany

1954 Switzerland
West Germany 3-2 Hungary
Runners up: Austria, Uruguay

1950 Brazil
Uruguay 2-1 Brazil
Runners up: no game

1938 France
Italy 4-2 Hungary
Runners up: Brazil, Sweden

1934 Italy
Italy 2-1 Czechoslovakia (ET)
Runners up: Germany, Austria

1930 Uruguay
Uruguay 4-2 Argentina
Runners up: no game

MISS ROSS ON THE SPOT

How fitting that the 1994 World Cup finals should end with a missed penalty — especially as they started with one!

At the opening ceremony in Chicago, a giant ball was placed on the penalty spot to be kicked just a few yards into an open goal. Unmissable you'd think. Not for the legendary soul singer Diana Ross. She hooked the ball sending it off to the left of the posts — the pre-programmed goalposts collapsed anyway.

Unbelievably the following year, Ross was at it again. This time at the opening of the Rugby League World Cup at Wembley Stadium. This time however, they didn't take the risk of asking her to kick a conversion.

ENGLAND MAKE GOOD — 16 YEARS LATER

Alf Ramsey played in one of the great upsets in English football history, but made amends by being manager of its greatest triumph.

He was part of the England team that suffered one of the biggest World Cup upsets ever, losing 1-0 to the fledgling USA in Belo Horizonte, Brazil in 1950. Such a shock was this defeat, many London newsroom sports desk writers genuinely believed that there was some kind of mistake with the machinery that had transmitted the information.

Ramsey did not forget the defeat. Thirteen years later, Ramsey became manager of the England team. When he took the job he predicted that England would win the next World Cup. Three years later his prediction came true. His masterful command of the game, a home crowd advantage and a squad full of talent allowed Ramsey to erase the bad memories of Belo Horizonte with a classic victory over West Germany in the 1966 World Cup final in London. He later confessed that he did not remember feeling any emotion at all. He said he was too busy watching and noting every movement to feel tense or excited.

football heroes

1) HUNGARY – 1954 WORLD CUP

They are the best team I ever played against.

Stanley Matthews

Hungary's 'Magical Magyars' are considered the greatest national team of all-time. Their attack was led by Puskas, the 'Galloping Major' and team captain. Partnering him was Kocsis 'the Golden Head'; Hidegkuti, the first player to perfect the deep-lying centre-forward role; Czibor, one of the greatest left-wingers of all-time; and Boszik, a graceful midfielder and master play maker. The team played a revolutionary formation, 4-3-3.

2) BRAZIL – 1958 WORLD CUP

Individually, the 1958 team was the most talented of my time.

Pelé

The 1958 Brazilian team was the only team that could match the Magical Magyars for skill and class. Brazil's line-up, boosting a 17-year-old Pelé and the devastating winger Garrincha, also included Didi, perhaps the greatest midfield tactician of all-time. Vava provided the team with the scoring touch and Zagalo the drive and balance. In defence, Brazil also had the world's best pair of full-backs in Djalma and Nilton Santos. Gilmar was the greatest goalkeeper the country has ever seen.

3) ENGLAND – 1966 WORLD CUP

They think it's all over… it is now!

Kenneth Wolstenholme,
BBC commentator

In 1966 all manager Alf Ramsey's predictions came true. The 1966 World Cup was England's finest moment. Captained by Bobby Moore, England's 'Wingless Wonders' dispatched Argentina and then Portugal to set up a final with West Germany at Wembley. With Hurst replacing Jimmy Greaves up front, England won 4-2 after extra time, Hurst scoring his third goal in the 120th minute.

4) BRAZIL – 1970 WORLD CUP

The 1970 Brazilian team had a forward line comprising Pelé, Jairzinho and Tostao. The midfield was run by the master-passer Gerson and Rivelino. While their defensive line up was weak in comparison, the strength of their attack guaranteed goals. Oddly, the team boasted three superb left-footers – Gerson, Rivelino and Tostao.

5) HOLLAND – 1974 WORLD CUP

Arguably the first team to master the 'Total Football' strategy, Holland was led by Cruyff in attack, Neeskens in midfield and Krol in defence. Their skill proved too much for most opposition – unless they were German.

SIZES OF FOOTBALL CROWDS

FA Cup final
Estimated 200,000 – Bolton v West
Ham 1923, Wembley

European Cup final
127,621 – Real Madrid v Eintracht
Frankfurt 1960, Hampden Park

World Cup
199,850 – Brazil v Uruguay 1950,
Maracana Stadium Brazil

World Cup qualifier
120,000 – Cameroon v Morocco
1981, Yaounde

Home international
149,547 – Scotland v England 1937,
Hampden Park

Scottish League
118,567 – Rangers v Celtic 1939,
Ibrox Park

Scottish Cup final
146,433 – Celtic v Aberdeen 1937,
Hampden Park

Football League
83,260 – Manchester United v
Arsenal 1948, Maine Road

British Club match
143,470 – Rangers v Hibs 1948,
Hampden Park

Premiership
67,758 – Manchester United
v Southampton 2004, Old Trafford

PERFORMANCE ANALYSIS

Total number of matches – 64

Games ending in a conclusive result at 90 mins – 45

% of games ending in a conclusive result at 90 mins – 70

Total number of drawn matches at 90 mins – 19

% of total number of drawn matches at 90 mins – 30

Number of games decided by the golden goal – 3

% of games decided by the golden goal – 19

Number of games decided by penalty shoot out – 2

% of games decided by penalty shoot out – 13

Total number of goals – 161

Goals to match ratio – 2.52

Total number of penalties – 13

Total number of own goals – 3

Total number of red cards – 17

Red cards to games ratio – 0.27

Total number of yellow cards – 266

Yellow cards to games ratio– 4.16

TOP SCORING TEAM

Brazil – 18

TEAM CONCEDING LEAST GOALS

Argentina – 2

TEAM CONCEDING MOST GOALS

Saudi Arabia – 12

HIGHEST SCORING MATCH

Group E

Germany 8-0 Saudi Arabia

HAT-TRICK HEROES

Miroslav Klose (Germany)

Pedro Pauleta (Portugal)

QUICKEST GOAL

11 seconds – Hakan Sükür (Turkey)

PENALTY SHOOT OUT RESULTS IN THE WORLD CUP

1982 – (SF) **Germany v France**	3-3	5-4	(6 shots each)
1986 – (QF) **Germany v Mexico**	0-0	4-1	(4 and 3 shots)
1986 – (QF) **France v Brazil**	1-1	4-3	(5 shots each)
1986 – (QF) **Belgium v Spain**	1-1	5-4	(5 shots each)
1990 – (2R) **Rep. Ireland v Romania**	0-0	5-4	(5 shots each)
1990 – (QF) **Argentina v Yugoslavia**	0-0	3-2	(5 shots each)
1990 – (SF) **Argentina v Italy**	1-1	4-3	(4 and 5 shots)
1990 – (SF) **West Germany v England**	1-1	4-3	(4 and 5 shots)
1994 – (2R) **Bulgaria v Mexico**	1-1	3-1	(4 shots each)
1994 – (QF) **Sweden v Romania**	2-2	5-4	(6 shots each)
1994 – (F) **Brazil v Italy**	0-0	3-2	(4 and 5 shots)
1998 – (2R) **Argentina v England**	2-2	4-3	(5 shots each)
1998 – (QF) **France v Italy**	0-0	4-3	(5 shots each)
1998 – (SF) **Brazil v Netherlands**	1-1	4-2	(4 shots each)
2002 – (2R) **Spain v Rep. Ireland**	1-1	3-2	(5 shots each)
2002 – (QF) **Korean Rep. v Spain**	0-0	5-3	(5 and 4 shots)

FIVE SUBBUTEO FACTS

More than 700 different strips have appeared on the figures

The annual Subbuteo World Cup was first held in 1987

Three black players were introduced in 1995 after complaints the game did not reflect the ethnic mix of football

More than 300,000 of the miniature teams were sold each year in the 1960s and 1970s

In 1987, Justin Finch, 16, ranked world fifth at Subbuteo, insured his right hand for £160,000

When France added the Euro 2000 title to their 1998 World Cup crown, they established themselves as one of the greatest sides of the late 1990s. It was a welcome turnaround for a nation whose team had, until then, been embarrassing underachievers.

On paper previous teams had been a dream. In midfield the team of the 1980s boasted the great Michel Platini as well as Jean Tigana and Alain Giresse, plus the enviable strike force of Dominique Rocheteau and Didier Six. So what went wrong? Arguably, the team was cursed with bad luck, not least in their 1982 World Cup semi-final clash with West Germany.

The game was a clash of styles; the classy French side pitching their talent against the German will to win.

Germany drew first blood, Pierre Littbarski smashing a volley beyond the grasp of French keeper Jean-Luc Ettori from 25 yards out (1-0). The French responded by laying siege to Harald Schumacher's goal. When Rocheteau went down in the box, Platini gave the German keeper no chance from the penalty spot (1-1).

The most controversial moment of the game came after half-time, when substitute Patrick Battiston bore down on the German goal. Schumacher came pounding off his line, colliding with the French defender, knocking him unconscious. The referee, Charles Corver, failed to produce a card or even award a free-kick. Battiston was taken to hospital.

The score remained locked at 1-1 as the match went into extra time. Within two minutes of the restart, Marius Trésor curled in a free kick from the right hand edge of the box (2-1). Alain Giresse made it 3-1, whipping the ball home for France.

But the match was far from overKarl-Heinz Rummenigge pulled a goal back for the Germans before Klaus Fischer brought the teams level again with an incredible bicycle kick goal in the 108th minute. It was down to a penalty shoot-out. France's skill would probably have won out in a re-match, but it was just their luck that the match ended with penalties. It was the first World Cup finals match to be decided on penalties. Sadly, the better, more attractive team lost. French defender Bossis' weak shot allowed Schumacher to make the all-important save. Horst Hrubesch took the last spot-kick for Germany. With unruffled efficiency. He scored (5-4). and Germany went into the final.

A tearful French side could barely absorb the defeat. 'If only we had realised how good we were,' Platini said later, 'we would never have lost that game.' Indeed.

YOU. HOME. NOW. THOSE THAT BLEW IT BEFORE
THE OPENING WHISTLE OF THE WORLD CUP

2002
Manchester United's Roy Keane stormed out of the Irish team's training camp in Saipan two weeks before the tournament began. Keane, who was captain, panned the side's preparations as amateurish in a row with coach Mick McCarthy. McCarthy sent him home.

2002
Uncapped Portuguese defender Daniel Kennedy was sent home after failing a drugs test before a warm-up match. A banned diuretic was found in his bloodstream.

1998
South African players Naughty Mokoena and Brendan Augustine were sent home from France. The hard-living pair had rolled back to their hotel at 5am, despite a strict team curfew of 10pm.

1994
After scoring a typically awe-inspiring goal against Greece, Maradona tested positive for the banned substance Ephedrine and was thrown out of the tournament.

In the same year, a Swiss referee, Kurt Rothlisberger, was sent home after failing to award Belgium a penalty in their second round defeat by Germany.

Meanwhile, German midfielder Steffen Effenberg was thrown out of the national squad after making an obscene gesture to the jeering German fans while being substituted.

Finally, Romanian Ioan Valdoiu was sent off for an altercation with a teammate after coming on as a substitute in a match against Switzerland. Ashamed of his antics, the Romanian football authorities insisted that he go home.

1978
Scottish winger Willie Johnston was sent home after testing positive for drugs following a defeat at the hands of Peru.

The solid gold Jules Rimet trophy was stolen while on exhibition at Central Hall in Westminster prior to the 1966 World Cup finals in London. Amazingly, it was found a few days later under a bush in a South London garden by a dog called Pickles.

Mexico, in 1986, became the first country to host the Cup twice after Colombia pulled out citing economic reasons.

The fastest goal in the World Cup finals was scored by Hakan Sükür for Turkey in their 3-2 win over South Korea in Daegu in 2002. It took him just 11 seconds!

Two players have scored in every match of the tournament to help their sides to victory. Alcide Ghaggia for Uruguay in Brazil in 1950 and Jairzinho of Brazil in Mexico in 1970.

Argentina's Pedro Monzon became the first player to be sent off in a World Cup final. He was dismissed against West Germany in Rome in 1990 for a tackle on Jürgen Klinsmann. It was a fiery Argentine squad, as team mate Gustavo Dezotti followed later in the match for pushing Jürgen Kohler. The team lost 1-0.

The last player to be sent off in a final was Marcel Desailly for a tackle on Cafu during France's 3-0 win over Brazil in Paris in 1998. Indeed Cafu is the first player ever to appear in three World Cup finals. He came on as a substitute against Italy in the 1994 final when Brazil won 3-0 on penalties in Los Angeles. He started in their 3-0 defeat by France in Paris in 1998 and led his country to a 2-0 win over Germany in Yokohama in Japan/South Korea in 2002.

He's pulling him off! The Spanish manager is pulling his captain off!

George Hamilton on Spain manager Luis Swarez's substituting of Emilio Butragueno during their World Cup qualifier

Football Legends

THE GODS WHO WALK AMONG US

THOSE WHO ALMOST SERVED –
CELEBS ON THE PITCH

Rod Stewart – Apprenticeship with Brentford
Nicky Byrne – Trainee goalkeeper for Leeds
Angus Deayton – Trial for Crystal Palace
Gordon Ramsay – Played for Glasgow Rangers, signed as a pro at 15
Bradley Walsh – Eight years as a pro at Brentford. Left because of injuries
Harvey (So Solid Crew) – Played for AFC Wimbledon
Julio Iglesias – Trial for Real Madrid
Luciano Pavarotti – Goalie for Modena, he became a singer after
a car crash ended his playing career

MAKING A SPLASH – SOME AMAZING DEBUTS

All footballers are nervous when they make their first team debut. The roar of the fans, the expectations of friends, family and management. Often players will have worked their way up to that first-team place all the way from a teenage apprenticeship. Others might have the financial expectations of a six-figure transfer fee to justify.

Some players have failed to shine on their debut, while others do just OK. Some end up committing terrible fouls and getting sent off. But some get it better than right and set the stadium on fire.

Jermaine Pennant scored three goals on his full Premiership debut for Arsenal in 2003. Alan Shearer also netted a hat trick in his debut. In his case for Southampton in a 4-2 win over Arsenal.

Stan Collymore was another who scored three times in his home debut for Leicester in a 5-2 victory over Sunderland in 2000, while Alan Davis made his Man U debut in the 1983 FA Cup final (no pressure, then). United beat Brighton 4-0 after a 2-2 draw.

Most of these players went on to enjoy solid careers for club and country, so pity then Henry Morris. Despite scoring a hat trick in his Scottish debut in an 8-2 win over Northern Ireland, it was to be his only international cap. Go figure.

TOTAL FOOTBALL – JOHAN CRUYFF

A fantastic footballer, compared in his time to Pelé, Johan Cruyff is these days best known for bringing an entirely different style of football to the masses – not simply for himself, but also for his whole team.

'Total Football' in itself isn't a new idea; it's been around since the 1950s, when it was known as 'The Whirl', but Cruyff brought the approach to the international stage in the 1970s. To work it needs a team of 10 players of equal ability who are comfortable in any position, thereby allowing any player at any point of the game, to switch into another role as the situation demands. Defenders become forwards, forwards become defenders. It may sound crazy, but it worked under Cruyff. Holland became one of the greatest sides of the decade under his captaincy.

Cruyff himself was, like his system, the total footballer. He would mainly play as an attacking midfielder, but would suddenly switch sides to confuse his markers or drop to defence in times of need. Such was his skill that in the 1974 World Cup, 15 of the Dutch goals either started or ended with the captain. His favourite trick, the 'Cruyff turn' was to flick the ball behind his own leg, turn to face the opposite direction, and then accelerate away from the hapless defender who was left trying to tackle at thin air.

BEERS MADE FOR FOOTBALL TEAMS

Ducket Ale **(Berwick Rangers)** – Made by Border breweries
for the club and named after a stand in the ground

Forever Bury Beer **(Bury)** – Brewed by The Leyden Brewery
which donates a percentage of profits to the club

Grecian Ale **(Exeter City)** – Brewed by Sharp's Breweries,
a percentage of sales goes to the club.

Goalden Hatter **(Luton Town)** – Brewed by Banks
and Taylor for the club's supporters.

football heroes

FAMOUS FOOTBALL MOVIES

Arsenal Stadium Mystery (1940)
Kes (1969)
Yesterday's Hero (1979)
Porridge (1979)
Gregory's Girl (1981)
Escape to Victory (1981)
ID (1994)
When Saturday Comes (1996)
Fever Pitch (1997)
The Match (1999)
Mike Bassett: England Manager (2001)
Shaolin Soccer (2001)
Bend it like Beckham (2002)

> **There's no way Ryan Giggs is another George Best.
> He's another Ryan Giggs.**
> ## Denis Law

BRAIN-BOX PLAYERS

Shaka Hislop – Degree in mechanical engineering; he apparently passed up the chance to work for NASA to pursue his football career.

Ian Dowie – Degree in Aeronautical Engineering and Masters in Mechanical Engineering.

Steve Coppell – Studied economics at Liverpool University.

Tony Adams – Sports Science degree from Brunel University.

Brian McClair – Studied for a maths degree while playing at Motherwell.

David Wetherall – Chemistry degree and representative at World Student Games in 1991.

Barry Horne – Degree in Chemistry.

Steve Palmer – MSc in computing from Oxbridge.

Socrates – Qualified paediatrician.

TOO MUCH CASH AND NOT ENOUGH FOOTBALL –
THE NORTH AMERICAN SOCCER LEAGUE

The rise and demise of the North American Soccer League is one of the weirdest tales in modern football. Essentially an effort to launch the game in the one major territory it had not conquered (America), the North American Soccer League (NASL) tried hard to succeed. It spent millions on star players and even Americanised the rules of the game but its financially top heavy structure didn't last. Formed out of two pro-soccer leagues in 1968 – the FIFA-sanctioned United Soccer Association and the unsanctioned National Professional Soccer League – NASL would fold just 16 years later.

NASL did have one success of note – the success of the New York Cosmos, the biggest club in the league, which drew upwards of 40,000 fans per game at its height. However, the average attendance of the other league teams never reached above 15,000.

NASL realised something had to be done and set about selling the sport of soccer to Americans, to whom the game was completely alien. It changed the rules to include more American sporting practices, such as a 35-yard line for offsides, and a shootout to decide matches that ended in a draw. It spent a fortune on high-profile foreign players – including Pelé, George Best, Gordon Banks, Franz Beckenbauer and Johan Cruyff – leaving the Americans on the bench and increasing rather than diminishing the foreign image of the sport.

The League's uncontrolled growth and rampant spending heralded its decline in 1984. But despite its ugly collapse, the NASL did manage to introduce the sport of soccer to the US. It is now one of the top participatory sports among kids in the US today.

> **I don't think there is anybody bigger or smaller than Maradona.**
> ## Kevin Keegan

football heroes

FORMER JOBS OF PRO FOOTIE PLAYERS

Gilberto Silva

Sweet manufacturer, quarry worker and furniture manufacturer. Took up odd jobs to support his family when his father died. His friends persuaded him to go back to football

Chris Waddle

Sausage stuffer

Dean Windass

Bricklayer

Barry Hayles

Carpenter

Steve Jones

Soap factory worker

Les Ferdinand

Delivery driver, plasterer's mate

Chris Armstrong

Bus Cleaner

Bob Wilson

PE teacher

FOOTBALLERS ON SCREEN

Vinnie Jones
Movies (*Lock, Stock and Two Smoking Barrels*, *Snatch*, *Gone in 60 Seconds*)

Bobby Moore
Movies (*Escape to Victory*)

Eric Cantona
Movies (*Elizabeth*), Ads (Nike)

Scott Parker
Adverts (for McDonalds, aged 14)

David Ginola
Adverts (for Head and Shoulders shampoo)

Pierluigi Collina
Adverts and pop videos. Collina was voted Italy's sexiest man after modelling during Milan fashion week

Jeff Astle
Crooned on Baddiel and Skinner's *Fantasy Football*

THE INDIVIDUAL — DIEGO MARADONA

When it comes to individual skill, nobody can rival Maradona. Despite being only 5ft 5in, he had incredible upper body strength which he combined with devastating bursts of pace and the exceptional close control of a supreme dribbler. When he made his run on goal, defenders simply couldn't get near him. It was no better for the keeper as Maradona finished with a shot like a canon.

But for all Maradona's talent, he seemed forever surrounded by controversy. This contrast was never more striking than in a 1986 World Cup quarter-final match against England. Early in the second half, he clearly punched the ball past England goalkeeper Peter Shilton. To England's dismay, the referee's angle on the ball was not clear enough; he was fooled by Maradona's claims of innocence. The illegal goal was allowed to stand. Maradona later infamously claimed that the goal was scored by 'the Hand of God'.

But four minutes later, he showed his true brilliance. He picked the ball up inside his own half and dribbled past five England players, including the goalkeeper, before slotting it home with the calm of a man playing in his own back yard.

In the same tournament, he would score two more fine individual goals in the semi-final against Belgium and his clever pass set up Argentina's winning goal in their 3-2 victory over West Germany in the final.

For all intents and purposes Maradona, the supreme individualist, had won the World Cup on his own.

**The talk in America is all about Disney's summer smash...
But Jürgen Klinsmann is the Lion King of Germany. He's a
predator, and his domain is the 18-yard box.**
John Motson during Germany v Belgium, USA 1994

football heroes

THE WORLD'S MOST EXPENSIVE PLAYER – ZINEDINE ZIDANE

Zinedine Zidane was born on 23 June 1972, in Marseilles. Zidane got his start in football at an early age making his debut for Cannes in the First Division at the tender age of 17. It was from this debut it became clear that football had gone from being an ambition to a passion for the young Frenchman. As a midfielder for Cannes he scored his first goal on 8 February 1991 (for which he received a Renault Clio from the Cannes President). His first season with the club was marked by their qualification for the UEFA Cup.

His move to Bordeaux in 1992 was hard on 20-year-old Zidane, but he adapted with flying colours. With Zidane on board, Bordeaux impressed in the French league and reached the final of the UEFA Cup in 1995-96.

After his four crucial seasons with Bordeaux, he moved to Juventus. It was with this mighty Italian team that Zidane began to win serious titles. They won the 1996 European Super Cup, the 1996 World Championship Cup and the 1997 European Super Cup. They won the Italian title in 1997 and 1998, and were Champions League finalists in 1997 and 1998. Zidane's awards included the Golden Ball in 1998 and FIFA World Player of the Year in 1998 and 2000.

But it was to be in 1998, and in his own country, that Zidane truly made his mark on the world. France were the hosts of the sixteenth World Cup. The French team were only given an outside chance of winning but to everyone's surprise they made it through to the final where they faced a tough challenge against the defending world champions and perennial victors, Brazil.

Zinedine Zidane's two headers stunned Brazil in the first half of the final at the Stade de France. These goals gave the French a 2-0 lead going into the break. A third goal was added by the team in the second half to win. The underdog French team had beaten the strongest team in the world and it was largely down to one man.

In 2001, Zizou's (as he became known to fans) incredible talent was emphasised in hard cash. He became the most expensive player in football history when Real Madrid acquired him for £46 million pounds. Cheap at the price.

THE SOCCER MOVIE TO END ALL SOCCER MOVIES – ESCAPE TO VICTORY

Escape to Victory is probably the most beloved football movie of all time. Not for the plot or the acting, which are both pretty rubbish, but for the stellar line-up of football legends who play cameo roles in this gung-ho feel-good footie romp.

The 1981 film is based on a true story. It is the tale of a football-mad German general in World War II who, on realising he has several pre-war football stars incarcerated in his POW camp, organises a match between the combined Allied forces and their German captors. The highly trained German team sees the game as an opportunity to prove the supremacy of the master race, the Allies see it as a chance to escape. The film climaxes at the game's half-time. The Allies must choose whether to steal away to freedom as planned or stay to give the Germans a good old-fashioned sporting hiding. Here is the line up of the team:

Allies

Robert Hatch (USA) *Sylvester Stallone*
Michael Fileu (BEL) *Paul Van Himst*
John Colby (ENG) *Michael Caine*
Pieter Van Beck (Hol) *Co Prins*
Doug Clure (ENG) *Russell Osman*
Terry Brady (ENG) *Bobby Moore*
Arthur Hayes (SCO) *John Wark*
Carlos Rey (ARG) *Ossie Ardiles*
Sid Harmor (ENG) *Mike Summerbee*
Luis Fernandez (BRA) *Pelé*
Erik Ball (DEN) *Søren Lindsted*

Subs

Paul Wolchek (POL) *Kazimierz Deyna*
Gunnar Hilsson (NOR) *Hallvar Thoresen*
Also Tony Lewis (IRE) *Kevin O'Callaghan*
(who broke his arm before the match)

Just for the record, the Allied team win and escape anyway, but in real life they also won but were all executed by their captors.

Michel Platini is one of the greatest play makers in the history of the game. Born in 1955 in Lorraine of French/Italian descent, Platini started his career at French club Nancy-Lorraine before moving on to Saint-Etienne, where he won the League in 1981. In 1982 he moved to Italian club side Juventus, where he would score an impressive 68 goals in 147 league games as a midfielder, and find himself the Serie A top goal scorer three times in a row. Platini helped the club win two League titles, plus the Italian Cup, the European Cup and the Cup Winners' Cup.

His effortless achievement continued at national level. Platini captained the French national team to European Championship honours in 1984. As always he led from the front, becoming the top scorer in the tournament with nine goals.

Football historians will remember Platini as one of the greatest passers of the ball in the game, and, despite being nominally a midfielder, a great creative attacking force. He was also a master of the free kick, accurate and powerful. It was a skill he built up through hours of practice using a row of dummies set up on the pitch during training.

Such was Platini's dominance of European football in the early 1980s that he was voted European Footballer of the Year an unprecedented three times in succession, in 1983, 1984 and 1985.

> **'Lord Nelson! Lord Beaverbrook! Sir Winston Churchill! Sir Anthony Eden! Clement Attlee! Henry Cooper! Lady Diana! Maggie Thatcher — can you hear me, Maggie Thatcher! Your boys took a hell of a beating! Your boys took a hell of a beating!'**
>
> Norwegian commentator Bjorn Lillelien at the final whistle of Norway's 2-1 win over England in 1981

MOST GOALS SCORED IN AN ENTIRE CAREER

1. Pelé – 1,282
2. Arthur Friedenreich – 1,239
3. Flavio – 1,025
4. Romário – 915 (and counting)
5. Dario – 926

IT'S AN UNFAIR COP – BOBBY MOORE GETS FITTED UP

Bobby Moore joined West Ham as a schoolboy and was a regular in the first team by 1960. He was a composed central defender, far removed from the tough-tackling hard men of the day. In 1964, he skippered West Ham to success in the FA Cup final at Wembley where they beat Preston North End 3-2, the first of three successive trips to the national stadium in major finals in as many years for Moore. He would be undefeated on each occasion.

In 1966, aged just 25, Moore was the leader of the side which gave English football its crowning glory and established him as true sporting icon. Although it was Geoff Hurst who scored the historic hat-trick that clinched the 4-2 World Cup final win over West Germany, it was Moore's inch-perfect passing that set up two of Hurst's goals. One of many timeless images from that day is of Moore gallantly wiping his hands on his shirt before shaking the Queen's hand as she presented him with the Jules Rimet Trophy.

But his reputation would be called into doubt when Moore led the England team in defending their World Cup title in Mexico in 1970. While conducting altitude training in Colombia, the captain was caught in a major stitch-up. He was accused of stealing a bracelet from a jeweller in Colombia, and arrested by the police. The charges were eventually dropped and Moore was exonerated. It was a cheap shot meant to unsettle the England captain and his team. It may have worked. England only got to the last eight, defeated by West Germany in extra time. It would be 12 years before England were to return to the World Cup finals.

football heroes

When an inquisitive journalist asked Celtic manager Jock Stein whether Kenny Dalglish's best position was in attack or in midfield, Stein replied: 'Och, just let him on the park.' That was the thing about Dalglish. He was so comfortable on the ball that he could have played anywhere.

A childhood Glasgow Rangers supporter, he actually started out playing in goal then switched to right half. He had trials with a number of clubs including Liverpool, who turned him down. A mistake which cost them £440,000 to rectify some years later.

The 16-year-old Dalglish joined Celtic in 1967. It took three years for him to establish himself in the first team, by which time Celtic were the undisputed kings of Scottish football. Many a defender tired to kick the slight Dalglish off the park only to discover he was a lot tougher (and faster) than he looked.

After collecting 10 major medals with Celtic and scoring 167 goals, he moved to Anfield in 1977 as a replacement for Kevin Keegan. Dalglish was an instant success, scoring 30 goals in his first season, among them the winner in the European Cup final at Wembley. He was voted Footballer of the Year in 1979 and 1983 and formed a formidable partnership with Ian Rush who would make incisive runs following passes from 'King Kenny'. These were the Red's glory years: five league titles, four league cups, two more European cups.

In 1985 Dalglish became player/manager and in his first season guided Liverpool to a League and Cup double — a feat that had eluded even the club's most successful managers Bill Shankley and Bob Paisley. Daglish was named Manager of the Year. Only a year earlier Daglish had witnessed the tragedy at Heysel. Sadly, in 1989, Daglish was still Liverpool boss at the Hillsborough disaster.

Dalglish hung up his boots in 1990 having become the first player ever to score a century of goals in both Scotland and England. For skill on the ball and for the sheer amount of silverware accrued as both a player and as a manager, Kenny Dalglish is one of the true soccer greats.

Pundit heroes

THE MEN BEHIND THE MICROPHONES

FORMER TEAMS OF TV PUNDITS

BBC
Gary Lineker – Tottenham Hotspur and England
Alan Hansen – Liverpool and Scotland
Ian Wright – Arsenal and England

ITV
Ally McCoist – Rangers and Scotland
Andy Townsend – Chelsea and Republic of Ireland
Robbie Earle – Wimbledon and England

THE SHOCKING DEATH OF ANDRÉS ESCOBAR

Colombia had a disastrous 1994 World Cup. After losing to Romania in the opening match of their group, the strong Colombian team needed at least a draw against the usually unimpressive US team to have a chance of progressing in the tournament. But in the 34th minute defender Andrés Escobar accidentally chipped the ball into his own net. The US went on to win the game 2-1 and Colombia were out.

Escobar remained unrepentant about the cock-up and told reporters: 'It's not the end of the world.'

The game was to prove equally traumatic for BBC pundit Alan Hansen. In the post-match analysis, Hansen was as unforgiving as the Colombian fans about Escobar's performance, stating angrily that the defender 'should be shot' for the own goal. As it turned out, he wasn't alone in this opinion.

As Escobar and his fiancée left a restaurant in a Medellín suburb 10 days later, three men held him against a wall and shot him in the face and chest 12 times, shouting 'goal' with each blast.

While rumours circulated that the murder was in reprisal for a failed betting scam run by Colombian drug cartels, the BBC issued a quiet apology for Hansen's remarks.

THE ORIGIN OF COLEMANBALLS

'For those of you listening in black and white, Hungary are playing in red shirts, white shorts and green socks, and attacking the goal to our left.'

So said David Coleman while commentating on the match between Hungary and Argentina in the 1978 World Cup for BBC Radio 4. Indeed it was Coleman who was to lend his name to the twisted phrases, malapropisms and double meanings that plague the words of all those who commentate on sports for a living.

Although known as one of televised football's leading commentators, Coleman began his career as an athlete. In 1949 he became the only non-international to win the Manchester Mile.

Unfortunately, injury put an end to his dream of continuing his career and Coleman turned to reporting on the *Country Press* in Cheshire, at 22, becoming one of the youngest editors in the country.

In 1954 he joined the BBC in Birmingham as a news assistant. He was appointed sports editor the following year before being picked by the head of sport, Peter Dimmock, to front the new sports magazine programme, *Grandstand*.

Since then he has covered many major sporting events and occasions, including 16 Olympic Games, eight Commonwealth Games and a whole host of World Cup football tournament. Such was his stature within the BBC that for many years he also presented the sports quiz *A Question of Sport* and *BBC Sports Personality of the Year*.

However he achieved a new level of fame when the satirical magazine, *Private Eye*, dedicated an affectionate column within its pages exclusively to his vocal gaffs. It was called 'Colemanballs'. Since then spotting these malappointed statements and cringeworthy mistakes has been a joy of sports fans everywhere.

At some point every working commentator from John Motson to Gary Lineker has made an appearance in 'Colemanballs' but one man stands head and shoulders above the rest for his misuse of the English language – Big Ron Atkinson. The author of such statements as 'Beckenbauer really has gambled all his eggs' and 'That boy throws a ball further than I go on holiday' has virtually invented his own language in the commentary box. Atkinson's is a world of 'lollipops', 'the second post', 'going full gun' and the 'Hollywood Ball'.

Whatever that means. Surely if one man ever deserved his own column, it's Atkinson. But will it happen? In the great man's own words: 'I'm going to make a prediction – it could go either way.'

> I've always said there's a place for the press, but they haven't dug it yet.
> **Tommy Docherty**

PREMIERSHIP PRIMA DONNAS

Peter Shilton
Perfectionist; he made teammates re-enact any goal he conceded over and over in training.

Emerson Moises Costa
Brazilian transfer who signed to Middlesbrough but fled to Rio as soon as the sun went in.

David Unsworth
Only plays for clubs that his wife approves of.

Alan Shearer
Insisted would only sign for Newcastle if he could wear the number '9' shirt and take penalties.

Graeme Le Saux
Chelsea defender who gets extremely furious when people suggest he's anything but happily married.

Paolo Futre
Stormed out of training when not given the number '10' shirt. Demanded to be substituted in a pre-season friendly as the opposition were 'tackling like maniacs'.

Vinnie Jones
Stormed out of QPR when Gerry Francis was appointed coach as he, clearly, fancied the job himself.

Pierre Van Hooijdonk
Earned the name 'Mr Popular' after refusing to play for Nottingham Forest claiming the team (he was signed to) wasn't good enough for the Premiership.

Joey Beauchamp
Got homesick when arrived at West Ham after travelling the 60 miles from native Swindon.

FIVE BOOKS BY FOOTBALL PUNDITS

Bob Wilson: My Autobiography – Bob Wilson

The Green Line – Alan Green

Motty's Year – John Motson

Gray Matters – Andy Gray

My Greatest Game – Bob Holmes

A PUNDIT'S FOUR-LETTER TIRADE

Have you ever wondered what your favourite commentators were really thinking? Following England's loss to Brazil in the 2002 World Cup finals, television viewers finally got to find out when the BBC accidentally broadcast comments made by commentators Alan Hansen and Ian Wright.

Digital viewers saw their screens go blank, but could still hear the panel, who believed themselves to be off air, discussing the game.

'Seaman was five yards off his line!' cried former England and Arsenal striker Ian Wright, expletives pouring out of his mouth. 'And what was he (referring to England coach Sven Goran Eriksson) doing taking Michael Owen off?'

The normally taciturn Alan Hansen was next to get himself into hot water when asked casually which match was coming up next. He cheerfully replied:

'It's the Krauts!'

A BBC spokesman later attributed the blunder to a 'technical fault'. A statement issued by the broadcaster read:

'Obviously Gary [Lineker], Alan, Peter [Reid] and Ian were unaware they were on air. It was a private conversation between friends and no offence was intended.'

Two years later a similar off air boo-boo cost former Manchester United and Aston Villa manager Ron Atkinson his broadcasting career, after some allegedly racist remarks about Chelsea's black defender Marcel Desailly following a Champions League game against Monaco.

TOTALLY HATSTAND – FOOTBALL'S FAVOURITE NUTTERS

David Icke
Coventry goalkeeper turned 'son of God'. Described by *The Guardian* as 'a lunatic on the political fringe. A true nutter if ever there was one.'

Imre Varadi
The joker. While at Everton, Vardi allegedly laid his manhood across the sleeping lips of Adrian Heath. Heath awoke and leapt up in horror, injuring himself and missing several matches.

Mark Dennis
Claimed if he hadn't been battering players on the pitch for Birmingham City, he would have been battering spectators on the terraces. True to his word, he was repeatedly sent off for his violent displays.

Frank McAvennie
Unashamed man about the pitch for Celtic and man about town for Page 3 girls everywhere. Once shrugged off accusations of drug taking with the line: 'och, it was only a wee bit o' Charlie.'

Neil Ruddock
Broke both of Andy Cole's legs in a Liverpool v Man U reserve match. Decked Robbie Fowler for tampering with his favourite shoes.

Diego Maradona
Eye-popping enthusiasm, cocaine, prostitutes, fights, performance enhancing drugs, shooting at journalists, depression, club management and his own leisure wear brand. The don of nutters.

Robin Friday
Had 'mild' and 'bitter' tattooed under his nipples. He is reported as taking to a dance floor in Reading in nothing but a fur coat and painting the walls of his room black to stop the 'crazy wallpaper patterns freaking him out'.

Marco Boogers
Sent off in his debut game. The big Dutchman found it hard to settle at West Ham. Finally declared 'psychologically unfit' by the team and went to live in a caravan in rural Holland.

Newcastle, of course, unbeaten in their last five wins.
Brian Moore

Bruce Grobbelaar
Famous for: Bungs, extrovert goal keeping and that moustache
But fans love him for: That wobbly legged penalty style

Stan Bowles
Famous for: Drugs, drink, women, but mainly gambling.
But fans love him for: The winning goal against Leeds in the final game of the 75/76 season that put QPR on top (for nine days)

Roberto Carlos
Famous for: Huge thighs and awesome free kicks
But fans love him for: A free kick directly into the goal from the corner flag

Jimmy Johnstone
Famous for: Booze and getting lost at sea
But fans love him for: Terrifying play against Leeds in European Cup semi-final in 1970

Duncan Mackenzie
Famous for: 40-a-day smoking habit
But fans love him for: Best player never selected for England

Jim Baxter
Famous for: The treble and double at Rangers. The scourge of the English
But fans love him for: Scottish 2-1 win at Wembley over England in 1963

Charlie George
Famous for: A North London hero with a truly terrible haircut
But fans love him for: His goal celebration at 1971 FA Cup final

Paul McGrath
Famous for: 'Training? I'm not a bloody sea lion'
But fans love him for: Boozing. Especially going AWOL before a World Cup qualifier against Albanian

So often the pendulum continues to swing with the side that has just pulled themselves out of the hole.

Tony Gubba

> **An icon of his generation, adored by millions across the globe, who has brought hope to his nation where there was once despair... and Nelson Mandela.**
> *The Guardian*, describing a meeting between David Beckham and South African president Nelson Mandela.

THAT LAUGH — IT CAN ONLY BE STUART HALL

While Stuart Hall may be most famous for laughing himself to the point of a hernia while watching Europeans fall over in foam fat suits on *It's a Knockout*, by trade, he is a football commentator. Nowadays he has returned to his original passion and can be heard on the microphone up in the stands for Radio Five Live.

Hall has been fanatical about football, and Manchester City in particular, since the age of seven. He even had a successful trial for the team and was offered professional terms of £20 a week in winter and £10 a week in summer. He declined, instead going into journalism.

Hall says the greatest match he ever witnessed was the 1977 clash at the Olympic Stadium in Rome between Borussia Mönchengladbach and Liverpool in the European Cup final. However the first match he ever commentated on he never saw.

'It was 1958,' recalls Hall. 'Sheffield Wednesday against Leicester City, and it finished 4-4. It was a great game but I didn't see anything of it, it was shrouded in fog. I had to make up my mind then whether to come clean and admit I hadn't seen anything, or make up all eight goals. I did the latter, I lied. I didn't see a single goal, but people thought I had ESP. And there was no television in those days so they were none the wiser!'

So now you know. Don't believe everything you hear.

JUST TIME FOR SOME LATE HEADLINES:
THE MATCH OF THE DAY TEAM IN FULL

Gary Lineker
England's second-highest goalscorer with 48 strikes in 80 games, Lineker won the Golden Boot at the World Cup in Mexico in 1986. He played for Leicester, Everton, Barcelona and Tottenham, where he won the FA Cup. He joined the BBC in 1995 and now presents *Match of the Day*.

Alan Hansen
One of the most successful British footballers ever, during Hansen's 14 years at Liverpool he won seven Championships, three European Cups, two FA Cups, four League Cups and one League Super Cup. He was also capped 26 times by Scotland. He has been a regular on *Match of the Day* since 1992.

Mark Lawrenson
Winner of five League titles, the European and FA Cups and three League Cups while at Liverpool, Lawrenson went on to manage Oxford United and work with Kevin Keegan at Newcastle. He has been a regular television pundit since 1997.

Gordon Strachan
Winner of League Championships north and south of the border, the European Cup Winners' Cup and 50 international caps, he took up his first managerial post at Coventry in 1996. He went on to take Southampton to the 2003 FA Cup final.

Peter Schmeichel
A world-class goalkeeper, in Schmeichel's eight-year stint at Old Trafford he collected five Championships, three FA Cups and captained the side in their 1999 Champions League win. Capped 128 times for Denmark, he won Euro 92 and reached the World Cup quarter-finals in 1998.

John Motson
'Motty' has been a member of *Match of the Day* for nearly 30 years. He joined the team as a 26-year-old and soon became one of its key commentators. Altogether John has covered over 1,000 matches for the BBC.

Alan Shearer
Began at Southampton before moving to Blackburn in 1992. Shearer's goals inspired the team to the 94/95 Premiership title. He moved to Newcastle in 1996. He is the Premiership's all-time record goalscorer, scoring his 200th goal against Charlton in 2002.

football heroes

SOME PREMIER LEAGUE MASCOTS

Arsenal – Gunnersaurus Rex (Dinosaur)

Aston Villa – Hercules Lion

Birmingham City – Beau Brummie (Bulldog)

Blackburn Rovers – Roar Lion

Bolton Wanderers – Lofty Lion

Charlton Athletic – Floyd and Harvey (Bears)

Chelsea – Stamford Lion

Crystal Palace – Alice The Eagle

Everton – Mr Toffee

Fulham – Terry Bytes (Computer)

Manchester City – Moonchester (Alien)

Manchester United – Fred The Red (Dog)

Middlesbrough – Roary Lion

Newcastle United – Monty Magpie

Norwich City – Captain Canary

Portsmouth – Nelson The Dog

Southampton – Super Saint (Dog)

Tottenham Hotspur – Chirpy Cockerel

West Bromwich Albion – Baggie Bird

Source: www.sports-mascots.co.uk

FOOTBALL'S RENAISSANCE MAN: JIMMY HILL DOES IT ALL

Jimmy Hill OBE is *the* British football personality. Instantly recognisable by his long chin, distinctive beard and forthright opinions, but what you may not know about our Jimmy is the incredible diversity of his career.

Hill started playing football professionally in 1949 with Brentford, before moving to Fulham in 1953. Four years later he would become chairman of the PFA (Professional Footballers' Association), successfully campaigning to scrap the Football League's £20 maximum wage. He retired from playing in 1961, joining Coventry City as manager and turning the team around from a Third Division to a First Division squad. After a move into broadcasting in 1967, Hill would return to Coventry City again in 1975, when he became managing director and then chairman of the club. In 1987, he became chairman of another former club; this time helping Fulham survive almost certain bankruptcy before laying the foundations for a Premiership team with the financial backing of Mohammed Al Fayed.

But Hill's contribution to football goes much further than this. Not only did he rid the game of the maximum wage, he commissioned the first all-seater stadium when at Coventry and has been credited with changing the point scoring system (to the three points for a win system currently in use today). A former player, union leader, coach, manager, director, chairman and sports presenter, Hill famously took over from an injured linesman in a match between Arsenal and Liverpool in 1972, stepping in as a match official so the game could continue.

He continues to hold a special position in the affections of the millions who have grown up with his punditry and shared in his passion for the game.

> **What I said to them at half-time would be unprintable on the radio.**
> ## Gerry Francis

MAD, BAD AND DANGEROUS ON SHOW. GAZZA IN THE PRESS

Throughout the early 1990s, the football skills of Paul Gascoigne dominated the football press. His inch-perfect crosses, incredible ball control, incisive breaks and above all footballing spirit made him one of the great midfielders of his era.

However through the early 1990s, the off and on pitch antics of Paul Gascoigne also dominated the tabloid press. Gazza's irrepressible sense of humour and borderline insanity set the red tops on fire with clockwork regularity. Here are few classic Gazza moments:

- **In 1990**, having won the hearts of the nation with his talent and tears in Italia 90, Gazza appears on the aeroplane steps on his arrival back in Blighty wearing a pair of outsized plastic breasts.

- **In 1992**, while playing for Lazio in Rome, Gazza is asked a question about the match by one of the country's most respected journalists. His answer is to burp into the microphone on Italian national television.

- **In 1993**, Gazza is in Norway for a vital World Cup qualifier, when he is asked by a local journalist if he has a message for the people of Norway. 'Yes, I do', he replied before announcing what he truly thought about the country.

- **In 1995**, Gazza marks his Rangers debut by scoring a breathtaking goal and then miming the flute playing of the Protestant Orangemen, hence inflaming hundreds of years of local religious conflict.

- **In 1998**, on the eve of the World Cup, and with the England manager vacillating as to whether to add Gascoigne to the squad, Gazza must prove his fitness. He does so by by being photographed on a 48-hour sleep-free booze bender with celebrity pals Danny Baker and Chris Evans, rounding the session off with an early morning doner kebab.

Way to go my son. Eccentric, flawed, maybe a little mad but a true football hero.

Five days shalt thou labour, as the Bible says. The seventh day is the Lord thy God's. The sixth day is for football.

Anthony Burgess

FURTHER READING

Addicted, Tony Adams
Bizarre Fantasy Football XIs, David Kohn
Blessed, George Best
Bobby Moore, Tina Moore
The Book of Bizarre Football, Graham Sharpe
The Book of Football Quotations, Peter Ball and Phil Shaw
Brian Glanville's Book of Footballers, Brian Glanville
The Football Factory, John King
Fantastic Football Facts, Nick Callow
Footballer's wives tell their tales, S Webb
Great Football Heroes, Geoff Tibballs
The Guinness Book of Football Blunders, Cris Freddi
'66: The Inside Story of England's 1966 World Cup Triumph, Roger Hutchinson

www.4thegame.co.uk
www.footballchants.org
www.football365.com
www.britishcouncil.org/japan-sport-footballculture.htm
www.footballlinks.net
www.longballgame.com
http://football-rumours.com
http://football.guardian.co.uk
http://skysports.planetfootball.com
www.TEAMNAME.rivals.net
www.sports-mascots.co.uk
www.sportsoffensive.com

INDEX

INDEX

In football, time and space are the same thing.

Graham Taylor